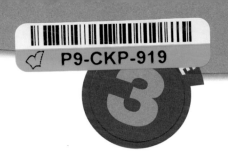

A BALANCED MATHEMATICS PROGRAM INTEGRATING SCIENCE AND LANGUAGE ARTS

Unit Resource Guide
Unit 13
Parts and Wholes

THIRD EDITION

KENDALL/HUNT PUBLISHING COMPANY
4050 Westmark Drive   Dubuque, Iowa 52002

A TIMS® Curriculum
University of Illinois at Chicago

UIC The University of Illinois
at Chicago

The original edition was based on work supported by the National Science Foundation under grant
No. MDR 9050226 and the University of Illinois at Chicago. Any opinions, findings, and conclusions
or recommendations expressed in this publication are those of the author(s) and do not necessarily
reflect the views of the granting agencies.

Letter Home

Parts and Wholes

Date: _____

Dear Family Member:

In this unit, your child will participate in activities to learn basic fraction concepts. Students will learn the meaning of numerator and denominator and use them to name fractions. (See the picture on this page.) They will work with pattern blocks to learn that the size of a fractional piece depends on the size of the whole. For example, one-half of a cupcake is much different from one-half of a wedding cake. They will solve problems that lead them to understand that the parts into which the whole is divided must be equal. That is, one-fourth is not just one of any four parts; it is one of four *equal* parts.

You can help your child at home:

- **Fraction Spotting.** Point out fractions in your daily life; for example, one-half of a bottle of soda pop. Discuss what the whole is and what the fraction means. If the whole is 2 liters of soda in the bottle, then $\frac{1}{2}$ of the bottle is 1 liter of soda.

- **Doubling and Halving Recipes.** Use recipes that require fractional amounts, such as $\frac{1}{2}$ cup sugar or $\frac{1}{4}$ teaspoon salt. If you halve or double a recipe, help your child determine what the final amounts will be.

What fraction of the students are wearing glasses?

- **Fraction Games.** During this unit your child will play games that involve fractions. Encourage your child to bring these games home to play.

- **Multiplication Facts.** Help your child practice the multiplication facts for the square numbers using the *Triangle Flash Cards*.

Thank you for helping your child understand and use fractions.

Sincerely,

_____

Carta al hogar

Partes y enteros

Fecha: _____

Estimado miembro de familia:

En esta unidad, su hijo/a participará en actividades para aprender los conceptos básicos sobre fracciones. Los estudiantes aprenderán el significado de los términos numerador y denominador y los usarán para nombrar fracciones. (Vea la ilustración en esta página.) Usarán bloques geométricos para aprender que el tamaño de una parte fraccional depende del tamaño del entero. Por ejemplo, medio pastelito no es lo mismo que medio pastel de boda. Resolverán problemas que les ayudarán a comprender que las partes en las que se divide el entero deben ser iguales. Es decir, un cuarto no es simplemente una de cuatro partes cualesquiera; es una de cuatro partes iguales.

¿Qué fracción de los estudiantes usa lentes?

Usted puede ayudar a su hijo/a en casa:

- **Hallar fracciones.** Señalen fracciones que encuentren en la vida cotidiana; por ejemplo, media botella de refresco. Hablen acerca de qué es el entero y qué significa una fracción. Si el entero es 2 litros de refresco, entonces $\frac{1}{2}$ botella es 1 litro de refresco.

- **Duplicar recetas y dividir recetas por la mitad.** Use recetas que requieran cantidades fraccionales, como $\frac{1}{2}$ taza de azúcar o $\frac{1}{4}$ de cucharita de sal. Si divide una receta por la mitad o la duplica, ayude a su hijo/a a determinar cuáles serán las cantidades finales.

- **Juegos con fracciones.** Durante esta unidad su hijo/a jugará juegos con fracciones. Anime a su hijo/a a llevar estos juegos a casa para jugarlos juntos.

- **Tablas de multiplicación.** Ayude a su hijo/a a practicar las tablas de multiplicación con números cuadrados usando las tarjetas triangulares.

Gracias por ayudar a su hijo/a a comprender y usar fracciones.

Atentamente,

Letter Home

Parts and Wholes

Date: _____

Dear Family Member:

In this unit, your child will participate in activities to learn basic fraction concepts. Students will learn the meaning of numerator and denominator and use them to name fractions. (See the picture on this page.) They will work with pattern blocks to learn that the size of a fractional piece depends on the size of the whole. For example, one-half of a cupcake is much different from one-half of a wedding cake. They will solve problems that lead them to understand that the parts into which the whole is divided must be equal. That is, one-fourth is not just one of any four parts; it is one of four *equal* parts.

You can help your child at home:

- **Fraction Spotting.** Point out fractions in your daily life; for example, one-half of a bottle of soda pop. Discuss what the whole is and what the fraction means. If the whole is 2 liters of soda in the bottle, then $\frac{1}{2}$ of the bottle is 1 liter of soda.

- **Doubling and Halving Recipes.** Use recipes that require fractional amounts, such as $\frac{1}{2}$ cup sugar or $\frac{1}{4}$ teaspoon salt. If you halve or double a recipe, help your child determine what the final amounts will be.

What fraction of the students are wearing glasses?

- **Fraction Games.** During this unit your child will play games that involve fractions. Encourage your child to bring these games home to play.

- **Multiplication Facts.** Help your child practice the multiplication facts for the square numbers using the *Triangle Flash Cards*.

Thank you for helping your child understand and use fractions.

Sincerely,

_____

Carta al hogar

Partes y enteros

Fecha: _____

Estimado miembro de familia:

En esta unidad, su hijo/a participará en actividades para aprender los conceptos básicos sobre fracciones. Los estudiantes aprenderán el significado de los términos numerador y denominador y los usarán para nombrar fracciones. (Vea la ilustración en esta página.) Usarán bloques geométricos para aprender que el tamaño de una parte fraccional depende del tamaño del entero. Por ejemplo, medio pastelito no es lo mismo que medio pastel de boda. Resolverán problemas que les ayudarán a comprender que las partes en las que se divide el entero deben ser iguales. Es decir, un cuarto no es simplemente una de cuatro partes cualesquiera; es una de cuatro partes iguales.

¿Qué fracción de los estudiantes usa lentes?

Usted puede ayudar a su hijo/a en casa:

- **Hallar fracciones.** Señalen fracciones que encuentren en la vida cotidiana; por ejemplo, media botella de refresco. Hablen acerca de qué es el entero y qué significa una fracción. Si el entero es 2 litros de refresco, entonces $\frac{1}{2}$ botella es 1 litro de refresco.

- **Duplicar recetas y dividir recetas por la mitad.** Use recetas que requieran cantidades fraccionales, como $\frac{1}{2}$ taza de azúcar o $\frac{1}{4}$ de cucharita de sal. Si divide una receta por la mitad o la duplica, ayude a su hijo/a a determinar cuáles serán las cantidades finales.

- **Juegos con fracciones.** Durante esta unidad su hijo/a jugará juegos con fracciones. Anime a su hijo/a a llevar estos juegos a casa para jugarlos juntos.

- **Tablas de multiplicación.** Ayude a su hijo/a a practicar las tablas de multiplicación con números cuadrados usando las tarjetas triangulares.

Gracias por ayudar a su hijo/a a comprender y usar fracciones.

Atentamente,

_____

Table of Contents

Unit 13
Parts and Wholes

Unit 13

Outline
Parts and Wholes

Unit Summary

Students investigate part-whole fractions by working with pattern blocks, solving word problems, playing games, and making and using paper models. Basic fraction concepts are emphasized; procedures are not. A fundamental idea in several activities is that the meaning of a fraction depends on what the whole is (e.g., half an inch is much less than half a mile). Other important ideas are that the whole must be divided into equal parts, that fractions can have more than one name, and that ordering fractions by size requires attention to both the numerator and denominator. The use of one-half as a benchmark for comparing fractions is emphasized. The utility of fractions in everyday life is highlighted in several activities and in the homework. The DPP for this unit provides practice with and assesses the multiplication facts for the square numbers.

Major Concept Focus

- fraction concepts
- multiple representations of fractions
- problem solving with fractions
- concept of whole
- part-whole fractions
- area model of fractions
- fractions of sets
- concept of addition of fractions
- comparing fractions
- equivalent fractions
- Game: finding a fraction of a number
- Game: comparing fractions
- practice and assessment of the multiplication facts for the square numbers

Pacing Suggestions

- Lesson 4 *Fraction Games* consists of two games that develop and practice fraction concepts. If the class plays both games, this lesson will take two class sessions.
- Lesson 5 *Fraction Problems,* an optional lesson, is a set of word problems involving fractions. These problems can be solved in class or assigned as homework throughout the unit. Since the lesson requires little teacher preparation, it is appropriate to leave for a substitute teacher.

Assessment Indicators

Use the following Assessment Indicators and the *Observational Assessment Record* that follows the Background section in this unit to assess students on key ideas.

A1. Can students represent fractions using pattern blocks and drawings?

A2. Can students identify fractional parts of a set?

A3. Can students partition shapes into given fractions?

A4. Can students identify the whole when given a fractional part of the whole?

A5. Do students recognize that fractional parts of a whole must have equal areas?

A6. Can students compare and order fractions using one-half as a benchmark?

A7. Do students demonstrate fluency with the multiplication facts for the square numbers?

Unit Planner

KEY: SG = Student Guide, DAB = Discovery Assignment Book, AB = Adventure Book, URG = Unit Resource Guide, DPP = Daily Practice and Problems, HP = Home Practice (found in Discovery Assignment Book), and TIG = Teacher Implementation Guide.

	Lesson Information	Supplies	Copies/Transparencies
Lesson 1 **Kid Fractions** URG Pages 18–27 SG Pages 180–181 DPP A–B HP Parts 4–5 *Estimated Class Sessions* **1**	**Activity** A group of students stands at the front of the class while the teacher presents a fraction based on some characteristic of the group. The rest of the class tries to determine what characteristic the teacher has in mind. **Math Facts** DPP Bit A reminds students to use the *Triangle Flash Cards: Square Numbers*. **Homework** 1. Assign the Homework section of the *Kid Fractions* Activity Pages. 2. Remind students to take home their flash cards to practice the square numbers at home. 3. Assign Parts 4 and 5 of the Home Practice.	• 1 envelope for storing flash cards per student	
Lesson 2 **What's 1?** URG Pages 28–39 SG Pages 182–184 DAB Page 199 DPP C–F *Estimated Class Sessions* **2**	**Activity** Students use pattern blocks to solve concept-of-unit problems. **Math Facts** DPP items D, E, and F provide practice with multiplication facts. **Homework** Assign the *Naming Wholes and Parts* Homework Page in the *Discovery Assignment Book*. Students do not need pattern blocks to complete this page. **Assessment** Assign the *Pattern Block Fractions* Assessment Blackline Master.	• pattern blocks (2 yellow hexagons, 10 green triangles, 5 blue rhombuses, and 4 red trapezoids) per student group • 1 resealable plastic bag per student group, optional • overhead pattern blocks	• 1 copy of *Pattern Block Fractions* URG Page 35 per student
Lesson 3 **Pizza Problems** URG Pages 40–51 SG Pages 185–187 DPP G–J HP Part 3 *Estimated Class Sessions* **2**	**Activity** Students solve word problems about sharing pizza fairly. These problems introduce basic fraction ideas. **Homework** 1. Assign the Homework section of the *Pizza Problems* Activity Pages. 2. Assign problems from the *Fraction Problems* Activity Pages (optional Lesson 5) as appropriate. 3. Assign Home Practice Part 3. **Assessment** Use the *Observational Assessment Record* to note students' abilities to represent fractions in pictures, words, and symbols.	• 1 pair of scissors per student	• 4 copies of *Ten Pizzas* URG Page 48 per student pair • 1 transparency of *Centimeter Grid Paper* URG Page 49, optional • 1 copy of *Observational Assessment Record* URG Pages 9–10 to be used throughout the unit

	Lesson Information	Supplies	Copies/ Transparencies
Lesson 4 **Fraction Games** URG Pages 52–60 SG Pages 188–189 DAB Pages 201–213 DPP K–L HP Parts 1–2 *Estimated Class Sessions* **1-2**	**Games** *FractionLand:* Students advance tokens along a path and answer various questions along the way. Finding a fraction of a number is stressed. *Fraction Problem Game:* Students compare two fractions and say a number sentence to move their pieces. **Math Facts** DPP Bit K is the quiz on the square numbers. **Homework** 1. Students play the games at home. 2. Assign Parts 1 and 2 of the Home Practice. **Assessment** 1. Use DPP Bit K to assess students' fluency with multiplication facts for the square numbers. 2. Use the *Observational Assessment Record* to document students' abilities to find fractions of sets and to compare and order fractions. 3. Transfer appropriate documentation from the *Observational Assessment Record* to students' *Individual Assessment Record Sheets.*	• 1 envelope for storing flash cards per student • 1 pair of scissors per student • 50 counters (e.g., connecting cubes or beans) per student • 1 game token per student • 1 clear plastic spinner (or pencil with paper clip) per student group	• 1 copy of *Individual Assessment Record Sheet* TIG Assessment section per student, previously copied for use throughout the year
Lesson 5 **Fraction Problems** URG Pages 61–65 SG Pages 190–191 *Estimated Class Sessions* **1**	OPTIONAL LESSON **Optional Activity** Students solve a set of problems involving fractions. **Homework** Assign some or all of the problems for homework.	• counters • 1 calculator per student • 1 clock face per student, optional	

Connections

A current list of literature and software connections is available at *www.mathtrailblazers.com*. You can also find information on connections in the *Teacher Implementation Guide* Literature List and Software List sections.

Literature Connections
Suggested Titles

- Adler, David. *Fraction Fun*. Holiday House, New York, 1997.
- Mathews, Louise. *Gator Pie*. Sundance Publishing, Littleton, MA, 1995. (Lesson 3)
- Pallotta, Jerry. *Apple Fractions*. Scholastic, Inc., New York, 2002.
- Stamper, Judith Bauer. *Go, Fractions*. Penguin Putnam Books for Young Readers, New York, 2003.

Software Connections

- *Math Arena* is a collection of math activities that reinforces many math concepts.
- *Math Munchers Deluxe* provides practice finding equivalent fractions in an arcade-like game.
- *Mighty Math Calculating Crew* poses short answer questions about number operations and money skills.
- *National Library of Virtual Manipulatives* website (http://matti.usu.edu) allows students to work with fractions using electronic versions of manipulatives including fraction circles, rectangles, bars, and number lines.

Teaching All Math Trailblazers Students

Math Trailblazers® lessons are designed for students with a wide range of abilities. The lessons are flexible and do not require significant adaptation for diverse learning styles or academic levels. However, when needed, lessons can be tailored to allow students to engage their abilities to the greatest extent possible while building knowledge and skills.

To assist you in meeting the needs of all students in your classroom, this section contains information about some of the features in the curriculum that allow all students access to mathematics. For additional information, see the Teaching the *Math Trailblazers* Student: Meeting Individual Needs section in the *Teacher Implementation Guide*.

Differentiation Opportunities in this Unit

Games

Use games to promote understanding of math concepts and to practice skills with children who need more practice.

- *FractionLand* from Lesson 4 *Fraction Games*
- *Fraction Problem Game* from Lesson 4 *Fraction Games*

Journal Prompts

Journal prompts provide opportunities for students to explain and reflect on mathematical problems. They can help both students who need practice explaining their ideas and students who benefit from answering higher order questions. Students with various learning styles can express themselves using pictures, words, and sentences. Teachers can alter journal prompts to suit students' ability levels. The following lesson contains a journal prompt:

- Lesson 2 *What's 1?*

Extensions

Use extensions to enrich lessons. Many extensions provide opportunities to further involve or challenge students of all abilities. Take a moment to review the extensions prior to beginning this unit. Some extensions may require additional preparation and planning. The following lessons contain extensions:

- Lesson 1 *Kid Fractions*
- Lesson 4 *Fraction Games*

Background
Parts and Wholes

This is the first of three third-grade fraction units. Part-whole fractions are the main focus, but fractions in measurement and division are also included. Since this unit is the first of three, we concentrate on students' explorations and strategies for completing problems, not on computation. As students complete the activities in the unit, look for and discuss the various methods students devise to solve problems.

Types of Fractions

Most fractions fall into one of the following categories:

- part-whole fractions
- the names of points on a number line
- indicated divisions
- pure numbers
- ratios
- probabilities
- measurements

A source of confusion for students is that the same symbols are used for all these kinds of fractions. For example, the symbol "$\frac{1}{2}$" can represent a part of an object (one-half of a pizza), a part of a collection (one-half of a class), a part of a unit of measurement (one-half inch), a ratio (one part milk to two parts flour), a probability (the chance of a fair coin showing heads), part of a distance (one-half of the way to Paducah), a pure number (the average of 0 and 1), and even a division (of 1 by 2).

Part-Whole Fractions

An example of a part-whole fraction is *three-fourths* in the statement, "Last night I ate three-fourths of a carton of ice cream." To understand what *three-fourths* means, it must be clear what the whole is: How big was the carton of ice cream? This is probably the single most important idea in this unit.

It is also important for students to understand that the parts into which the whole is divided must be equal. The parts must have the same area, mass, or number. Many children think that any division into two parts is a division into halves; this is revealed by such statements as "I want the bigger half." Many activities in this unit involve this notion of sharing (or dividing) into equal parts, or "fair shares."

Sometimes, however, students carry this equality of parts idea too far. For example, when sharing money, it is not important that each person get the same number of bills and coins; all that matters is that everyone gets the same value of money. Similarly, if a rectangle is divided into fourths, the fourths may or may not have the same shape, but they must have the same area.

The whole in a part-whole fraction can be either a single thing (a pizza) or a collection (a class of students). When the whole is a single thing, the fairness of the shares depends on some measurable quantity (length, area, mass, etc.). Often, the area is the variable that must be equally allocated among the parts. Such a situation can be called an area model for fractions. When the whole is a collection, then counting is generally used to make fair shares. This unit includes wholes that are single things and wholes that are collections.

Multiple Representations

Another important idea in this unit is multiple representations of fractions and making connections between those representations. Fractions can be represented in words, symbols, pictures, or real objects. It is especially important for students to be able to move freely among these representations. Given symbols for a fraction, can students draw a picture or conceive of a realistic situation for that fraction? Can students explain the relationship between a group of five girls and two boys and the fraction $\frac{5}{7}$?

Given a fraction represented by a pattern block, can students identify the whole?

Fractions are commonly written with either a slash (1/2) or "stacked" ($\frac{1}{2}$). Both ways are correct although, at times, one or the other may be clearer. In our materials, we use both ways so students will recognize both.

Fractions as Quantities

Other ideas in this unit include putting fractions in order by size, recognizing that many names can refer to the same fraction (i.e., equivalent fractions) and estimating sums of fractions. Specific procedures for solving such problems, however, are not included. Rather, students use their basic understanding of the meaning of fractions as quantities to work through the problems. When students have a firm grasp on fractions as quantities, then learning the procedures will be quicker and deeper.

Observational Assessment Record

A1 Can students represent fractions using pattern blocks and drawings?

A2 Can students identify fractional parts of a set?

A3 Can students partition shapes into given fractions?

A4 Can students identify the whole when given a fractional part of the whole?

A5 Do students recognize that fractional parts of a whole must have equal areas?

A6 Can students compare and order fractions using one-half as a benchmark?

A7 Do students demonstrate fluency with the multiplication facts for the square numbers?

A8 _____

Name	A1	A2	A3	A4	A5	A6	A7	A8	Comments
1.									
2.									
3.									
4.									
5.									
6.									
7.									
8.									
9.									
10.									
11.									
12.									
13.									

Name	A1	A2	A3	A4	A5	A6	A7	A8	Comments
14.									
15.									
16.									
17.									
18.									
19.									
20.									
21.									
22.									
23.									
24.									
25.									
26.									
27.									
28.									
29.									
30.									
31.									
32.									

Unit 13

Daily Practice and Problems
Parts and Wholes

A DPP Menu for Unit 13

Two Daily Practice and Problems (DPP) items are included for each class session listed in the Unit Outline. A scope and sequence chart for the DPP is in the *Teacher Implementation Guide*.

Icons in the Teacher Notes column designate the subject matter of each DPP item. The first item in each class session is always a Bit and the second is either a Task or Challenge. Each item falls into one or more of the categories listed below. A menu of the DPP items for Unit 13 follows.

N Number Sense	✖ Computation	🕐 Time	⬡ Geometry
E, G–J, L	E	C, L	B

Math Facts	$ Money	🎼 Measurement	▱ Data
A, D–F, K		B	

Practicing and Assessing the Multiplication Facts

By the end of third grade, students are expected to demonstrate fluency with the multiplication facts. Students developed strategies for learning the multiplication facts in Units 3–10. In Unit 11, they began the systematic, strategies-based study of these facts. In this unit, students practice and are assessed on the multiplication facts for the square numbers. The *Triangle Flash Cards: Square Numbers* are in the *Discovery Assignment Book*

immediately following the Home Practice. DPP items A, D, E, and F provide practice with multiplication facts for the square numbers. Bit K is a quiz on the square numbers.

For information on the distribution and study of the multiplication facts in Grade 3, see the DPP Guide for Units 3 and 11. For a detailed explanation of our approach to learning and assessing the math facts in Grade 3, see the *Grade 3 Facts Resource Guide* and for information for Grades K–5, see the TIMS Tutor: *Math Facts* in the *Teacher Implementation Guide*.

Students may solve the items individually, in groups, or as a class. The items may also be assigned for homework. The DPPs are also available on the Teacher Resource CD.

Student Questions	Teacher Notes

 Triangle Flash Cards: Square Numbers

With a partner, use your *Triangle Flash Cards* to quiz each other on the multiplication facts for the square numbers. One partner covers the corner containing the highest number with his or her thumb. The second person multiplies the two uncovered numbers.

Separate the used cards into three piles: those facts you know and can answer quickly, those you can figure out with a strategy, and those you need to learn. Practice the last two piles again and then make a list of the facts you need to practice at home for homework.

Circle the facts you know and can answer quickly on your *Multiplication Facts I Know* chart.

TIMS Bit

The *Triangle Flash Cards* follow the Home Practice for this unit in the *Discovery Assignment Book*. Students should take them home for practice.

Have students record the facts they know well on their *Multiplication Facts I Know* chart. Since these charts can also be used as multiplication tables, students should have them available to use as needed.

Inform students when you will give the quiz on the square numbers. This quiz appears in Bit K.

Geoboard Area

Find the area of these shapes.

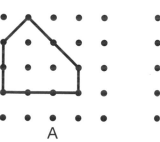  

A   B   C

One square unit

A. $6\frac{1}{2}$ square units

B. 6 square units

C. 9 square units; The shape is made up of a rectangle and a triangle. The rectangle's area is 8 square units. The triangle is $\frac{1}{2}$ of a 2 square-unit rectangle; its area is 1 square unit.

 Time Counting

Count by "15 minutes" from 7:00 A.M. to 7:00 P.M. Begin like this: 7 o'clock, 7:15, 7:30, 7:45, 8:00, 8:15 . . .

TIMS Bit

Work with a clock, showing the position of the minute hand as students count.

D **Square Care**

Help Professor Peabody fill in the missing information on his "Exploring Square Numbers" chart from Unit 11 Lesson 3.

Number on a side	Number in Square	Multiplication Fact
2	4	2 × 2 = 4
3	⬭	3 × 3 = 9
⬭	16	4 × 4 = 16
5	25	⬭
6	⬭	6 × 6 = ⬭
7	⬭	7 × ⬭ = 49
⬭	64	8 × 8 = ⬭
9	⬭	9 × 9 = ⬭

TIMS Task

Ask students what strategies they use for finding the missing information.

Number on a side	Number in Square	Multiplication Fact
2	4	2 × 2 = 4
3	9	3 × 3 = 9
4	16	4 × 4 = 16
5	25	5 × 5 = 25
6	36	6 × 6 = 36
7	49	7 × 7 = 49
8	64	8 × 8 = 64
9	81	9 × 9 = 81

E **Multiplying with Ending Zeros**

A. 5 × 5 =

B. 5 × 50 =

C. 8 × 8 =

D. 8 × 80 =

E. 2 × 2 =

F. 2 × 20 =

G. 4 × 4 =

H. 4 × 40 =

I. 40 × 40 =

J. 40 × 400 =

What patterns do you see?

TIMS Bit

A. 25	B. 250
C. 64	D. 640
E. 4	F. 40
G. 16	H. 160
I. 1600	J. 16,000

The answer is the product of the two non-zero numbers plus the number of zeros in the two factors.

F **How Many Times More**

A. Shana lives 6 blocks from her grandmother. Manuel lives six times as far from his grandmother. How far does Manuel live from his grandmother?

B. Ivor's family bought 3 books at the book fair. Gwen's family bought 3 times as many books at the book fair. How many books did Gwen's family buy at the book fair?

C. Karen is 7 years old. Her father is seven times as old. How old is Karen's father?

D. Write a story about 9×9.

TIMS Task

A. 36 blocks

B. 9 books

C. 49 years old

D. Stories will vary.

G **Kid Fractions**

Mrs. Marsh asked several students to stand. Then she asked the following questions.

1. What fraction of the students are wearing gym shoes?

2. What fraction of the students have brown eyes?

3. What fraction of the students are wearing a blue shirt?

4. What fraction of the students are girls?

TIMS Bit

Ask 6–8 students to stand up. Then, ask Questions 1–4 or ask students to make up their own fractions about them.

H   Numerators and Denominators

1. I am a fraction. My denominator is 8. My numerator is 5. Write me down and draw pictures that show
(a) one whole, and (b) me.

2. I am a fraction. My denominator is 2. My numerator is 3. Write me down, and draw pictures that show
(a) one whole, and (b) me.

TIMS Task

1. Asking for separate diagrams that show one whole and the fraction stresses the role of the unit. A possible drawing is:

(a) 1

(b) $\dfrac{5}{8}$

2. A possible drawing is

(a)

(b)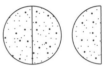

I   Fraction Skip Counting

Skip count by 1/2s to 10. You can use a diagram like this:

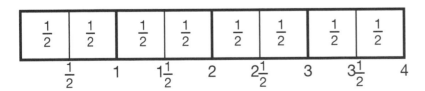

Skip count by 1/4s to 10.

TIMS Bit

More or Less Than $1\frac{1}{2}$

1. I am $\frac{1}{2}$ more than $1\frac{1}{2}$. What number am I?

2. I am $\frac{1}{4}$ less than $1\frac{1}{2}$. What number am I?

3. I am $\frac{1}{4}$ more than $1\frac{1}{2}$. What number am I?

TIMS Task

1. 2

2. $1\frac{1}{4}$

3. $1\frac{3}{4}$

Diagrams like those suggested in Bit I are helpful.

 Quiz on the Square Numbers

A. $4 \times 4 =$ B. $7 \times 7 =$

C. $1 \times 1 =$ D. $10 \times 10 =$

E. $3 \times 3 =$ F. $5 \times 5 =$

G. $6 \times 6 =$ H. $8 \times 8 =$

I. $9 \times 9 =$ J. $2 \times 2 =$

TIMS Bit

This quiz is on the third group of multiplication facts, the square numbers. We recommend 1 minute for this test. Allow students to change pens or pencils after the time is up and complete the remaining problems in a different color.

After students take the test, have them update their *Multiplication Facts I Know* charts.

 Time Fractions

How many minutes in

1. 1 hour?

2. $\frac{1}{4}$ hour?

3. $\frac{1}{2}$ hour?

4. $\frac{3}{4}$ hour?

5. $1\frac{1}{2}$ hours?

Use a clock and a calculator to help you.

TIMS Task

1. 60 minutes

2. 15 minutes

3. 30 minutes

4. 45 minutes

5. 90 minutes

Lesson 1

Kid Fractions

Lesson Overview

A group of students stands at the front of the class while the teacher presents a fraction based on some characteristic of the group. The rest of the class tries to determine what characteristic the teacher has in mind. Discussion focuses on the relationship between the part and whole and the meaning of the numerator and denominator.

Key Content

- Connecting mathematics with real-world situations.
- Finding a fractional part of a set.

Key Vocabulary

- denominator
- numerator

Math Facts

DPP Bit A reminds students to use the *Triangle Flash Cards: Square Numbers*.

Homework

1. Assign the Homework section of the *Kid Fractions* Activity Pages.
2. Remind students to take home their flash cards to practice the square numbers at home.
3. Assign Parts 4 and 5 of the Home Practice.

Curriculum Sequence

Before This Unit

Fractions

Students explored fractions in Grade 2 Units 14 and 20.

After This Unit

Fractions

Students will work with decimal fractions in Unit 15 *Decimal Investigations*. They will study common fractions again in Unit 17 *Wholes and Parts*.

Materials List

Supplies and Copies

Student	Teacher
Supplies for Each Student • envelope for storing flash cards	**Supplies**
Copies	**Copies/Transparencies**

All blackline masters including assessment, transparency, and DPP masters are also on the Teacher Resource CD.

Student Books
Kid Fractions (*Student Guide* Pages 180–181)
Triangle Flash Cards: Square Numbers (*Discovery Assignment Book* Page 197)

Daily Practice and Problems and Home Practice
DPP items A–B (*Unit Resource Guide* Pages 12–13)
Home Practice Parts 4–5 (*Discovery Assignment Book* Page 195)

Note: Classrooms whose pacing differs significantly from the suggested pacing of the units should use the Math Facts Calendar in Section 4 of the *Facts Resource Guide* to ensure students receive the complete math facts program.

A. Bit: Triangle Flash Cards:
Square Numbers (URG p. 12)

With a partner, use your *Triangle Flash Cards* to
quiz each other on the multiplication facts for the
square numbers. One partner covers the corner
containing the highest number with his or her
thumb. The second person multiplies the two
uncovered numbers.

Separate the used cards into three piles: those facts
you know and can answer quickly, those you can
figure out with a strategy, and those you need to
learn. Practice the last two piles again and then
make a list of the facts you need to practice at home
for homework.

Circle the facts you know and can answer quickly on
your *Multiplication Facts I Know* chart.

B. Task: Geoboard Area (URG p. 13)

Find the area of these shapes.

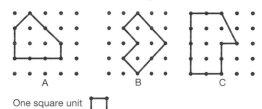

One square unit

Student Guide - page 180 (Answers on p. 26)

Teaching the Activity

The *Kid Fractions* Activity Pages in the *Student Guide* illustrate a group of students in Mrs. Bond's class. Use them to introduce the game or as follow-up. To begin, ask a group of students to come to the front of the class. Explain that you are going to write a fraction on the board that describes something shared by some of this group. For example, suppose you ask three girls and two boys to come to the front. Then, you write $\frac{3}{5}$ on the board as a fraction that shows the part of this group that are girls. The task of the class is to guess the characteristic you based the fraction on. As students guess, discuss whether each proposed characteristic fits the fraction or not.

Create several different fractions for the first group. For example, $\frac{2}{5}$ of the group described in the previous paragraph are male. Other attributes you might use to generate fractions are the type or color of shoes, clothing, or hair, or the wearing of eyeglasses. You can even combine attributes—$\frac{2}{5}$ of the group above might be girls with eyeglasses.

Introduce the terms *numerator* and *denominator*. In a fraction such as $\frac{2}{5}$, the 5 is the **denominator.** It tells the number of equal parts in the whole. The 2 is the **numerator.** It tells the number of parts being considered.

Then have a different number of students come to the front. Ask what the denominator of the fractions for this group is and why. Continue creating fractions as before. Highlight the importance of the whole in comparing fractions. For example, $\frac{1}{2}$ of a group of six students is not the same as $\frac{1}{2}$ of a group of eight students. The meaning of the fraction comes from knowing how many students are in the whole group.

As you play the game, you will have more opportunities to talk about the terms *numerator* and *denominator*. Continue to emphasize that the denominator gives the number of parts into which the whole is divided while the numerator tells how many of those parts you are interested in.

Content Note

Point out that fractions can be presented either with numerator and denominator separated by a diagonal line, such as 2/3, or stacked, such as $\frac{2}{3}$.

Continue the activity with many different groupings so that students experience fractions with different denominators.

You can also discuss equivalent fractions, especially fractions equivalent to one-half. Equivalent fractions, however, are usually not easy for children, so keep them simple. Suppose, for example, there are six students, three wearing eyeglasses. Either fraction—$\frac{3}{6}$ or $\frac{1}{2}$—fits the part of the group wearing glasses. The fraction $\frac{3}{6}$ can be interpreted to mean that three out of six students are wearing glasses. The fraction $\frac{1}{2}$ can be interpreted to mean that out of two equal groups of students one group has glasses. Write "$\frac{3}{6} = \frac{1}{2}$" to emphasize that either fraction can be used to describe the part of the group with glasses.

At this point, introduce the issue of the relative size of different fractions. Suppose you have two girls and four boys at the front. You can write "$\frac{2}{6} < \frac{4}{6}$" to show that there are fewer girls than boys. Suppose three out of six students are wearing red, and two out of six students are wearing blue. Some students may say that $\frac{3}{6} > \frac{2}{6}$. Other students, knowing that $\frac{3}{6} = \frac{1}{2}$ may instead say that $\frac{1}{2} > \frac{2}{6}$. Putting fractions in order by size builds a very important understanding of fractions as quantities rather than just symbols.

Math Facts

DPP Bit A gives instructions for using the *Triangle Flash Cards: Square Numbers*.

Homework and Practice

- Assign the Homework section of the *Kid Fractions* Activity Pages in the *Student Guide*.

- Remind students to practice the multiplication facts for the square numbers at home using their *Triangle Flash Cards*.

- DPP Task B provides practice finding area by counting square units.

- Part 4 of the Home Practice provides computation practice using money and Part 5 provides practice with multidigit addition and subtraction.

Answers for Parts 4 and 5 of the Home Practice are in the Answer Key at the end of this lesson and at the end of this unit.

Homework

Write your answers to the following "family fractions" questions.

1. Draw a picture of the people in your family. Then write several fractions for parts of your family. Explain each fraction. For example, if you live with your mother and two younger sisters, then you can write $\frac{1}{4}$ for the fraction of your family that is grown up: one of the four people in your family is an adult.

2. Draw a picture of some objects around your house. Then write several fractions for parts of the group. Explain each fraction. For example, suppose you have five cans of soup—three tomato and two chicken noodle. Then you could write $\frac{2}{5}$ for the fraction of the cans that are tomato.

3. About what fraction of the utensils (forks, knives, spoons) in your house are forks?

Kid Fractions   SG • Grade 3 • Unit 13 • Lesson 1 **181**

Student Guide - page 181 (Answers on p. 26)

Assessment

Through whole-class discussion, you can assess your class's familiarity with basic fraction concepts including (1) the importance of the whole in determining the size of a fraction, (2) connections between real situations and fraction symbols and words, (3) equivalent fractions, and (4) ordering fractions by size.

Extension

Use the picture of the students in Mrs. Bond's class (or a group of students at the front of your class) for a "Kid Fractions Contest" that awards points for original fractions that fit that group. The other students work in pairs for several minutes to generate fractions that fit the group. Then pairs share the fractions and attributes they have generated. A point is awarded for each original attribute. Come up with your own scoring scheme to determine what is original.

Name _____ Date _____

PART 3

Use a clock and a calculator to help you solve these problems.

How many minutes are there in:

1. 2 hours? _____

2. $1\frac{1}{2}$ hours? _____

3. $1\frac{1}{4}$ hours? _____

4. $1\frac{3}{4}$ hours? _____

5. $2\frac{1}{2}$ hours? _____

PART 4

Use what you know about quarters and $\frac{1}{4}$s to solve these problems. Tell how much money you would have after adding or subtracting these amounts.

1. You have 25¢ more than $2.50. _____

2. You have 25¢ less than $2.50. _____

3. You have 50¢ more than $2.50. _____

4. You have $1.50 more than $3.50. _____

5. You have $2.00 less than $3.75. _____

PART 5

Solve the problems. Estimate to be sure your answers are reasonable.

1. 4006
   +498

2. 4006
   −498

3. 7032
   +1777

4. 7032
   −1779

5. Explain your estimation strategy for Question 2.

PARTS AND WHOLES   DAB • Grade 3 • Unit 13 **195**

Discovery Assignment Book - page 195 (Answers on p. 27)

Name _____ Date _____

Triangle Flash Cards: Square Numbers

- Work with a partner. Each partner cuts out the flash cards.
- Your partner chooses one card at a time and covers the shaded number.
- Multiply the two uncovered numbers.
- Divide the cards into three piles: those facts you know and can answer quickly, those you can figure out with a strategy, and those you need to learn.
- Practice the last two piles again. Then make a list of the facts you need to practice at home.
- Repeat the directions for your partner.

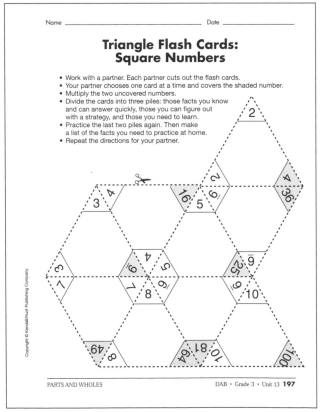

PARTS AND WHOLES   DAB • Grade 3 • Unit 13 **197**

Discovery Assignment Book - page 197

Estimated Class Sessions

1

At a Glance

Math Facts and Daily Practice and Problems

DPP Bit A reminds students to use the *Triangle Flash Cards: Square Numbers*. Task B reviews finding area.

Teaching the Activity

1. Discuss the questions on the first *Kid Fractions* Activity Page in the *Student Guide*.
2. Ask a group of students to come to the front of the class.
3. Write a fraction on the board that describes a certain part (attribute) of this group.
4. The class guesses the characteristic of the group that the fraction represents.
5. Describe the first group of students with several different fractions.
6. Have different numbers of students come to the front and continue creating fractions.
7. Discuss the terms *numerator*, *denominator*, *part*, and *whole* as the opportunity arises during the game.
8. Discuss equivalent fractions and compare fractions when appropriate.

Homework

1. Assign the Homework section of the *Kid Fractions* Activity Pages.
2. Remind students to take home their flash cards to practice the square numbers at home.
3. Assign Parts 4 and 5 of the Home Practice.

Extension

Have a "Kid Fractions Contest" using the picture of Mrs. Bond's students or a group of your own students.

Answer Key is on pages 26–27.

Notes:

Kid Fractions

Mrs. Bond's class is playing *Kid Fractions*. These students are at the front:

Mrs. Bond has written the fraction $\frac{4}{6}$ for a certain part of this group. The class is trying to guess what Mrs. Bond has in mind.

1. Could Mrs. Bond be thinking of the fraction that are boys?

2. What do you think Mrs. Bond is thinking?

3. Next, Mrs. Bond wrote the fraction $\frac{3}{6}$. Can you guess what she is thinking? Is there a second possibility?

4. Can you think of some other fractions that fit parts of this group? Make a list of fractions for these students. Tell why each fraction fits some part of the group.

180   SG • Grade 3 • Unit 13 • Lesson 1   Kid Fractions

Student Guide - page 180

Student Guide (p. 180)

Kid Fractions

1. No, $\frac{3}{6}$ of the students are boys.

2. $\frac{4}{6}$ of the students do not wear glasses, $\frac{4}{6}$ have pants on, etc.

3. $\frac{3}{6}$ of the students are boys; $\frac{3}{6}$ are girls; $\frac{3}{6}$ are wearing blue, etc.

4. Answers will vary. Some possibilities are: $\frac{1}{2}$ are boys, $\frac{1}{2}$ are girls, $\frac{5}{6}$ have dark hair, $\frac{1}{6}$ have freckles, $\frac{2}{6}$ have skirts on, etc.

Homework

Write your answers to the following "family fractions" questions.

1. Draw a picture of the people in your family. Then write several fractions for parts of your family. Explain each fraction. For example, if you live with your mother and two younger sisters, then you can write $\frac{1}{4}$ for the fraction of your family that is grown up: one of the four people in your family is an adult.

2. Draw a picture of some objects around your house. Then write several fractions for parts of the group. Explain each fraction. For example, suppose you have five cans of soup—three tomato and two chicken noodle. Then you could write $\frac{3}{5}$ for the fraction of the cans that are tomato.

3. About what fraction of the utensils (forks, knives, spoons) in your house are forks?

Kid Fractions   SG • Grade 3 • Unit 13 • Lesson 1   181

Student Guide - page 181

Student Guide (p. 181)

Homework

All three questions will have answers that vary. Students can have a discussion comparing the various fractions they find in their homes.

Discovery Assignment Book (p. 195)

Home Practice*

Part 4

I. $2.75

2. $2.25

3. $3.00

4. $5.00

5. $1.75

Part 5

I. 4504

2. 3508

3. 8809

4. 5253

5. Possible strategy: $4000 - 500 = 3500$.

Name _____ Date _____

PART 3

Use a clock and a calculator to help you solve these problems.

How many minutes are there in:

1. 2 hours? _____

2. $1\frac{1}{2}$ hours? _____

3. $1\frac{1}{4}$ hours? _____

4. $1\frac{3}{4}$ hours? _____

5. $2\frac{1}{2}$ hours? _____

PART 4

Use what you know about quarters and $\frac{1}{4}$s to solve these problems. Tell how much money you would have after adding or subtracting these amounts.

1. You have 25¢ more than $2.50. _____

2. You have 25¢ less than $2.50. _____

3. You have 50¢ more than $2.50. _____

4. You have $1.50 more than $3.50. _____

5. You have $2.00 less than $3.75. _____

PART 5

Solve the problems. Estimate to be sure your answers are reasonable.

1.   4006   2. 4006   3. 7032   4. 7032
    +498   −498   +1777   −1779

5. Explain your estimation strategy for Question 2.

PARTS AND WHOLES   DAB • Grade 3 • Unit 13 **195**

Discovery Assignment Book - page 195

---

*Answers for all the Home Practice in the *Discovery Assignment Book* are at the end of the unit.

Lesson 2

What's 1?

Lesson Overview

Estimated Class Sessions

2

Using pattern blocks, students explore the concept of a unit whole. They name fractions when given one whole and identify the whole when given a fraction.

Key Content

- Identifying the fraction for a given quantity when a unit whole is given.
- Identifying the unit whole when a fraction is given.
- Representing fractions using pattern blocks.
- Comparing and ordering fractions using the benchmark fraction one-half.

Key Vocabulary

- hexagon
- rhombus
- trapezoid
- unit whole

Math Facts

DPP items D, E, and F provide practice with multiplication facts.

Homework

Assign the *Naming Wholes and Parts* Homework Page in the *Discovery Assignment Book*. Students do not need pattern blocks to complete this page.

Assessment

Assign the *Pattern Block Fractions* Assessment Blackline Master.

After This Unit

Using Pattern Blocks to Represent Fractions

Students represent fractions using different manipulatives in Grades 3, 4, and 5. However, pattern blocks are used in all three grades. In Grade 3, when the yellow hexagon is one whole, students can represent halves, thirds, and sixths. In Grade 4, students add fourths to their set of pattern blocks and use them to

expand concepts from third grade and solve problems. In Grade 5, students add twelfths and use the pattern blocks to develop skills and concepts including finding equivalent fractions, representing whole numbers and improper fractions, and comparing fractions. They also use pattern blocks to develop procedures for adding, subtracting, and multiplying fractions.

Materials List

Supplies and Copies

Student	Teacher
Supplies for Each Student Group • pattern blocks (2 yellow hexagons, 10 green triangles, 5 blue rhombuses, and 4 red trapezoids) • resealable plastic bag, optional	**Supplies** • overhead pattern blocks
Copies • 1 copy of *Pattern Block Fractions* per student (*Unit Resource Guide* Page 35)	**Copies/Transparencies**

All blackline masters including assessment, transparency, and DPP masters are also on the Teacher Resource CD.

Student Books
What's 1? (*Student Guide* Pages 182–184)
Naming Wholes and Parts (*Discovery Assignment Book* Page 199)

Daily Practice and Problems and Home Practice
DPP items C–F (*Unit Resource Guide* Pages 13–15)

Note: Classrooms whose pacing differs significantly from the suggested pacing of the units should use the Math Facts Calendar in Section 4 of the *Facts Resource Guide* to ensure students receive the complete math facts program.

Daily Practice and Problems

Suggestions for using the DPPs are on page 33.

C. Bit: Time Counting (URG p. 13)

Count by "15 minutes" from 7:00 a.m. to 7:00 p.m. Begin like this: 7 o'clock, 7:15, 7:30, 7:45, 8:00, 8:15 . . .

E. Bit: Multiplying with Ending Zeros (URG p. 14)

A. $5 \times 5 =$ B. $5 \times 50 =$

C. $8 \times 8 =$ D. $8 \times 80 =$

E. $2 \times 2 =$ F. $2 \times 20 =$

G. $4 \times 4 =$ H. $4 \times 40 =$

I. $40 \times 40 =$ J. $40 \times 400 =$

What patterns do you see?

D. Task: Square Care (URG p. 14)

Help Professor Peabody fill in the missing information on his "Exploring Square Numbers" chart from Unit 11 Lesson 3.

Number on a side	Number in Square	Multiplication Fact
2	4	$2 \times 2 = 4$
3		$3 \times 3 = 9$
	16	$4 \times 4 = 16$
5	25	
6		$6 \times 6 =$
7		$7 \times \bigcirc = 49$
	64	$8 \times 8 =$
9		$9 \times 9 =$

F. Task: How Many Times More (URG p. 15)

A. Shana lives 6 blocks from her grandmother. Manuel lives six times as far from his grandmother. How far does Manuel live from his grandmother?

B. Ivor's family bought 3 books at the book fair. Gwen's family bought 3 times as many books at the book fair. How many books did Gwen's family buy at the book fair?

C. Karen is 7 years old. Her father is seven times as old. How old is Karen's father?

D. Write a story about 9×9.

Before the Activity

Check to be sure you have enough pattern blocks of each color so that every student group can have one full set for completing both the *What's 1?* Activity Pages and the *Pattern Block Fractions* Assessment Page. Or, organize the pattern blocks into sets and store them in resealable plastic bags.

Teaching the Activity

Begin by asking:

- *Do you think one-half is very large?*
- *Is half a million dollars a lot of money?*
- *Is halfway to the moon a large distance?*

Use the first page of the *What's 1?* Activity Pages in the *Student Guide* to start a discussion. The page presents a scenario in which a young boy is boasting to two friends that he can eat half a pizza. One child thinks the boy is eating a lot of pizza, but the other child realizes that one-half can be a lot or a little depending on the size of the whole pizza. Each of the ideas presented here introduces the basic idea of the activity: the role of the **unit whole.**

After the brief introduction, students can work through the *What's 1?* Activity Pages in small groups or pairs. Lead the class through any of the problems on those pages by using pattern block pieces on the overhead projector as needed. However, as much as possible, let the students attempt the problems within their groups.

Question 1 asks students to compare sizes and determine the fractional relationships between the various pattern block pieces. These questions are a warm-up for looking at fractional parts of a unit whole.

Questions 2–3 present problems in which students are given the whole and must find the fraction (part). Some of these questions also ask students to determine whether the fractions they identify are more than or less than one-half. *Questions 2E–2F* ask students to write fractions. Model writing fractions by discussing the numerators and denominators.

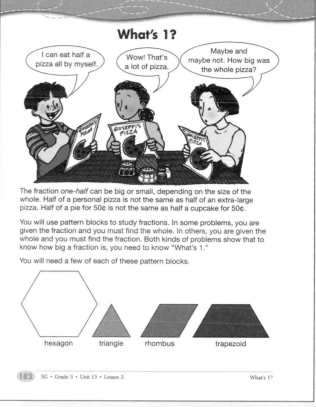

Student Guide - page 182

Covering Pattern Blocks

1. Look at all your pieces to answer these questions.
   A. How many red pieces cover one yellow?
   B. How many blues cover one yellow?
   C. How many greens cover one yellow?
   D. How many greens cover one blue?
   E. How many greens cover one red?
   F. Use two different colors to cover one red. What did you use?

Wholes to Parts

2. If the yellow hexagon is one whole, then
   A. What piece is one-half?
   B. What piece is one-third?
   C. What piece is one-sixth?
   D. We can write $\frac{2}{6}$ for 2 greens. Write a number for 5 greens.
   E. Write a number for 2 blues.
   F. Write a number for 3 reds.
   G. Write a number for 4 reds.
   H. Is 1 blue more or less than one-half?
   I. Are 2 blues more or less than one-half?

3. This shape is one whole.

   A. How many blues cover the shape?
   B. How many greens cover the shape?
   C. What piece is one-half?
   D. What piece is one-fourth?
   E. Write a fraction for 3 greens.
   F. What other piece makes the same fraction as 3 greens?
   G. Is 1 red more or less than one-half?

What's 1?   SG • Grade 3 • Unit 13 • Lesson 2   183

Student Guide - page 183 (Answers on p. 36)

Parts to Wholes

4. If the green piece is one-half, what piece is one whole?

5. If the blue is one-third, what is one whole?

6. Trace pattern blocks on a sheet of paper to answer these questions. For example, if the green is 1/3, draw one whole.

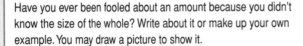

   If △ = $\frac{1}{3}$, then △△△ = 1 whole.

   A. If the green is 1/3, draw 2/3.
   B. If the green is 1/5, draw one whole.
   C. If the red is 1/3, draw one whole.
   D. If the yellow is 1/2, draw one whole.
   E. If the blue is 1/4, draw 3/4.

7. The green shape to the right is one whole.
   A. How many greens cover the shape?
   B. Write a fraction for 1 green.
   C. Write a fraction for 4 greens.
   D. Write a fraction for 7 greens.
   E. Write a fraction for 5 greens.

8. The green shape to the right is one whole.
   A. How many blues cover the whole?
   B. Write a fraction for 1 blue.
   C. Write a different fraction for 1 blue.
   D. Write a fraction for 1 red.
   E. Write a fraction for 1 yellow.
   F. Is 1 yellow more or less than one-half?

9. A. If the blue piece is one whole, write a number for 3 greens.
   B. If the blue piece is one whole, write a number for 1 yellow.

184   SG • Grade 3 • Unit 13 • Lesson 2   What's 1?

Student Guide - page 184 (Answers on p. 37)

Journal Prompt

Have you ever been fooled about an amount because you didn't know the size of the whole? Write about it or make up your own example. You may draw a picture to show it.

Questions 4–5 name a pattern block as a fraction and students must then determine the unit whole.

Question 6 asks students to make drawings using pattern blocks. *Question 6B* asks students to draw one whole if a green pattern block is one-fifth. Note that there are many different shapes that can be drawn with five green pieces.

Questions 7–8 use a six-sided shape (hexagon) that is divided into tenths for one whole. Ask students to identify the shape by name. Students are to determine the fraction for various given parts of the unit whole. For example, because ten greens cover the whole, one green is $\frac{1}{10}$. They will encounter similar questions on the *Pattern Block Fractions* Assessment Blackline Master, so be sure students understand the line of questioning. *Question 7E* asks students to write a fraction for five greens. Students may name either $\frac{1}{2}$ or $\frac{5}{10}$. Accept both answers and point out that the two fractions are equivalent.

Questions 8B and *8C* ask students to write two different fractions for one blue. Since one blue equals two greens, the fractions are $\frac{1}{5}$ and $\frac{2}{10}$. The order in which the students give these answers does not matter. To answer *Questions 8D* and *8E* they must see that since three greens cover one red and six greens cover one yellow, then one red equals $\frac{3}{10}$ and one yellow equals $\frac{6}{10}$.

Question 9 asks students to write fractions greater than one. Point out that if the blue piece is one whole, three greens is greater than one. We can write $\frac{3}{2}$ or $1\frac{1}{2}$.

Math Facts

DPP items D, E, and F provide practice with the multiplication facts for the square numbers.

Homework and Practice

- Assign the *Naming Wholes and Parts* Homework Page in the *Discovery Assignment Book*. *Questions 1–5* ask students to identify parts to wholes and wholes to parts. *Questions 6–10* are about the fraction one-half.

- DPP Bit C provides practice with time by skip counting by 15 minute intervals.

Assessment

The *Pattern Block Fractions* Assessment Blackline Master contains problems that are similar to the *What's 1?* Activity Pages in the *Student Guide*. Students need the same set of pattern blocks as before, so if you do not have enough sets for individual students, then make this assessment a group effort.

Name _____ Date _____

Naming Wholes and Parts
Homework

Solve the following problems.

1. Stephanie, Simon, and Caroline want to share this leftover pizza fairly. Draw how much pizza each person should get.

2. If this ◜ is one whole, then draw one-third.

3. If this ▭ is one-half, then draw one whole.

4. If this ▭ is one-fourth, then draw $\frac{3}{4}$.

5. If this ▭ is $\frac{1}{2}$ of a bar, draw the whole bar.

The next few problems are about a very important fraction, one-half. Use the back of this page for your answers.

6. Show one-half using a rectangle.
7. Show one-half using a circle.
8. Make up a story problem with one-half in it.
9. List some fractions that equal one-half.

What's 1?   DAB · Grade 3 · Unit 13 · Lesson 2 **199**

Discovery Assignment Book - page 199 *(Answers on p. 38)*

At a Glance

Math Facts and Daily Practice and Problems

DPP items D, E, and F provide practice with multiplication facts. For Bit C students skip count by 15 minute intervals.

Teaching the Activity

1. Ask students whether one-half is a large number, and use the first page of the *What's 1?* Activity Pages in the *Student Guide* to start a discussion of the role of the unit whole.
2. Students work through the *What's 1?* Activity Pages in small groups.

Homework

Assign the *Naming Wholes and Parts* Homework Page in the *Discovery Assignment Book*. Students do not need pattern blocks to complete this page.

Assessment

Assign the *Pattern Block Fractions* Assessment Blackline Master.

Answer Key is on pages 36–39.

Notes:

Pattern Block Fractions

You will need some of the yellow, green, blue, and red pattern blocks.

1. If the red trapezoid is one whole, then write a number for

    A. 1 green _____ **B.** 2 greens _____

    C. 1 blue _____ **D.** 1 yellow _____

    E. Is 1 blue more or less than one-half? _____

2. This shape is one whole.

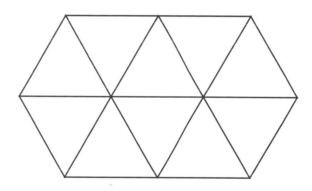

    A. How many greens cover this shape? _____

    B. Write a fraction for 3 greens. _____

    C. Are 3 greens more or less than one-half? _____

    D. Write a fraction for 1 red. _____

    E. Write a fraction for 5 greens. _____

    F. Write a different fraction for 5 greens. _____

    G. Is 1 red more or less than one-half? _____

3. If 1 green is one-eighth, draw a shape for one whole.
    Draw your shape on the back of this paper.

Student Guide (p. 183)

Covering Pattern Blocks

1. Look at all your pieces to answer these questions.
   A. How many red pieces cover one yellow?
   B. How many blues cover one yellow?
   C. How many greens cover one yellow?
   D. How many greens cover one blue?
   E. How many greens cover one red?
   F. Use two different colors to cover one red. What did you use?

Wholes to Parts

2. If the yellow hexagon is one whole, then
   A. What piece is one-half?
   B. What piece is one-third?
   C. What piece is one-sixth?
   D. We can write $\frac{2}{6}$ for 2 greens. Write a number for 5 greens.
   E. Write a number for 2 blues.
   F. Write a number for 3 reds.
   G. Write a number for 4 reds.
   H. Is 1 blue more or less than one-half?
   I. Are 2 blues more or less than one-half?

3. This shape is one whole.

   A. How many blues cover the shape?
   B. How many greens cover the shape?
   C. What piece is one-half?
   D. What piece is one-fourth?
   E. Write a fraction for 3 greens.
   F. What other piece makes the same fraction as 3 greens?
   G. Is 1 red more or less than one-half?

What's 1?   SG • Grade 3 • Unit 13 • Lesson 2   183

Student Guide - page 183

What's 1?*

1. A. 2 reds
   B. 3 blues
   C. 6 greens
   D. 2 greens
   E. 3 greens
   F. 1 blue and 1 green

2. A. 1 red
   B. 1 blue
   C. 1 green
   D. $\frac{5}{6}$
   E. $\frac{2}{3}$
   F. $1\frac{1}{2}$ or $\frac{3}{2}$
   G. 2 or $\frac{4}{2}$
   H. less
   I. more

3. A. 2 blues
   B. 4 greens
   C. 1 blue
   D. 1 green
   E. $\frac{3}{4}$
   F. 1 red
   G. more

*Answers and/or discussion are included in the Lesson Guide.

Student Guide (p. 184)

Parts to Wholes*

4. 1 blue

5. 1 yellow

6. A. Shapes may vary.

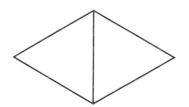

B.

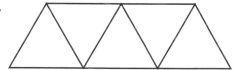

C.

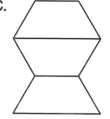

D.

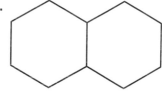

E.

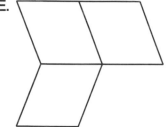

Parts to Wholes

4. If the green piece is one-half, what piece is one whole?

5. If the blue is one-third, what is one whole?

6. Trace pattern blocks on a sheet of paper to answer these questions. For example, if the green is 1/3, draw one whole.

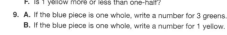

If  $= \frac{1}{3}$, then = 1 whole.

A. If the green is 1/3, draw 2/3.
B. If the green is 1/5, draw one whole.
C. If the red is 1/3, draw one whole.
D. If the yellow is 1/2, draw one whole.
E. If the blue is 1/4, draw 3/4.

7. The green shape to the right is one whole.
A. How many greens cover the shape?
B. Write a fraction for 1 green.
C. Write a fraction for 4 greens.
D. Write a fraction for 7 greens.
E. Write a fraction for 5 greens.

8. The green shape to the right is one whole.
A. How many blues cover the whole?
B. Write a fraction for 1 blue.
C. Write a different fraction for 1 blue.
D. Write a fraction for 1 red.
E. Write a fraction for 1 yellow.
F. Is 1 yellow more or less than one-half?

9. A. If the blue piece is one whole, write a number for 3 greens.
B. If the blue piece is one whole, write a number for 1 yellow.

184 SG • Grade 3 • Unit 13 • Lesson 2   What's 1?

Student Guide - page 184

7. A. 10 greens

    B. $\frac{1}{10}$

    C. $\frac{4}{10}$ or $\frac{2}{5}$

    D. $\frac{7}{10}$

    E. $\frac{5}{10}$ or $\frac{1}{2}$

8. A. 5 blues

    B. $\frac{2}{10}$ or $\frac{1}{5}$

    C. $\frac{1}{5}$ or $\frac{2}{10}$

    D. $\frac{3}{10}$

    E. $\frac{6}{10}$ or $\frac{3}{5}$

    F. more

9. A. $1\frac{1}{2}$ or $\frac{3}{2}$

    B. 3

*Answers and/or discussion are included in the Lesson Guide.

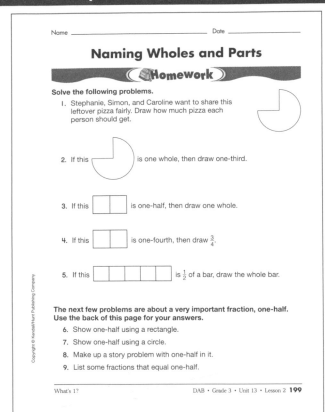

Name _____ Date _____

Naming Wholes and Parts

Homework

Solve the following problems.

1. Stephanie, Simon, and Caroline want to share this leftover pizza fairly. Draw how much pizza each person should get.

2. If this [image] is one whole, then draw one-third.

3. If this [image] is one-half, then draw one whole.

4. If this [image] is one-fourth, then draw $\frac{3}{4}$.

5. If this [image] is $\frac{1}{2}$ of a bar, draw the whole bar.

The next few problems are about a very important fraction, one-half. Use the back of this page for your answers.

6. Show one-half using a rectangle.

7. Show one-half using a circle.

8. Make up a story problem with one-half in it.

9. List some fractions that equal one-half.

What's 1?   DAB • Grade 3 • Unit 13 • Lesson 2 **199**

Discovery Assignment Book - **page 199**

Discovery Assignment Book (p. 199)

Naming Wholes and Parts

1.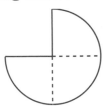

2.

3.

4. [image]

5. [image]

6. [image]

7.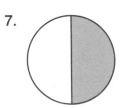

8. Answers will vary.

9. Answers will vary. Some fractions are: $\frac{2}{4}, \frac{3}{6}, \frac{5}{10}, \frac{10}{20}, \frac{50}{100}$.

Unit Resource Guide (p. 35)

Pattern Block Fractions

1. A. $\frac{1}{3}$

   B. $\frac{2}{3}$

   C. $\frac{2}{3}$

   D. 2

   E. more

2. A. 10 greens

   B. $\frac{3}{10}$

   C. less

   D. $\frac{3}{10}$

   E. $\frac{5}{10}$ or $\frac{1}{2}$

   F. $\frac{1}{2}$ or $\frac{5}{10}$

   G. less

3. Answers will vary. Here is one example.

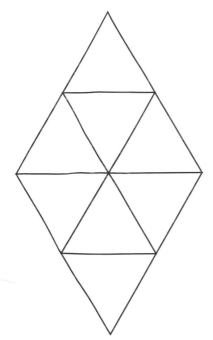

Name _____ Date _____

Pattern Block Fractions

You will need some of the yellow, green, blue, and red pattern blocks.

1. If the red trapezoid is one whole, then write a number for

   A. 1 green _____   B. 2 greens _____

   C. 1 blue _____   D. 1 yellow _____

   E. Is 1 blue more or less than one-half? _____

2. This shape is one whole.

   A. How many greens cover this shape? _____

   B. Write a fraction for 3 greens. _____

   C. Are 3 greens more or less than one-half? _____

   D. Write a fraction for 1 red. _____

   E. Write a fraction for 5 greens. _____

   F. Write a different fraction for 5 greens. _____

   G. Is 1 red more or less than one-half? _____

3. If 1 green is one-eighth, draw a shape for one whole. Draw your shape on the back of this paper.

Copyright © Kendall/Hunt Publishing Company

Assessment Blackline Master   URG • Grade 3 • Unit 13 • Lesson 2   35

Unit Resource Guide - page 35

Pizza Problems

Lesson Overview

Estimated Class Sessions
2

Students work in groups to solve problems about sharing pizza. They cut out paper circles to represent the pizza and use them to find what fraction of a pizza each person gets. Answers are recorded in pictures, words, and symbols.

Key Content

- Recognizing that fractional parts of a whole must have equal areas.
- Using an area model for part-whole fractions.
- Representing fractions using pictures, words, and symbols.
- Solving problems involving fractions.

Homework

1. Assign the Homework section of the *Pizza Problems* Activity Pages.
2. Assign problems from the *Fraction Problems* Activity Pages (optional Lesson 5) as appropriate.
3. Assign Home Practice Part 3.

Assessment

Use the *Observational Assessment Record* to note students' abilities to represent fractions in pictures, words, and symbols.

Materials List

Supplies and Copies

Student	Teacher
Supplies for Each Student • scissors	**Supplies**
Copies • 4 copies of *Ten Pizzas* per student pair (*Unit Resource Guide* Page 48)	**Copies/Transparencies** • 1 transparency of *Centimeter Grid Paper,* optional (*Unit Resource Guide* Page 49) • 1 copy of *Observational Assessment Record* to be used throughout this unit (*Unit Resource Guide* Pages 9–10)

All blackline masters including assessment, transparency, and DPP masters are also on the Teacher Resource CD.

Student Books
Pizza Problems (*Student Guide* Pages 185–187)

Daily Practice and Problems and Home Practice
DPP items G–J (*Unit Resource Guide* Pages 15–17)
Home Practice Part 3 (*Discovery Assignment Book* Page 195)

Note: Classrooms whose pacing differs significantly from the suggested pacing of the units should use the Math Facts Calendar in Section 4 of the *Facts Resource Guide* to ensure students receive the complete math facts program.

Assessment Tools
Observational Assessment Record (*Unit Resource Guide* Pages 9–10)

Daily Practice and Problems

Suggestions for using the DPPs are on page 45.

G. Bit: Kid Fractions (URG p. 15)

Mrs. Marsh asked several students to stand. Then she asked the following questions.

1. What fraction of the students are wearing gym shoes?
2. What fraction of the students have brown eyes?
3. What fraction of the students are wearing a blue shirt?
4. What fraction of the students are girls?

I. Bit: Fraction Skip Counting (URG p. 16)

Skip count by 1/2s to 10. You can use a diagram like this:

$\frac{1}{2}$	$\frac{1}{2}$	$\frac{1}{2}$	$\frac{1}{2}$	$\frac{1}{2}$	$\frac{1}{2}$	$\frac{1}{2}$	$\frac{1}{2}$

$\frac{1}{2}$ 1 $1\frac{1}{2}$ 2 $2\frac{1}{2}$ 3 $3\frac{1}{2}$ 4

Skip count by 1/4s to 10.

H. Task: Numerators and Denominators (URG p. 16)

1. I am a fraction. My denominator is 8. My numerator is 5. Write me down and draw pictures that show
   (a) one whole, and (b) me.
2. I am a fraction. My denominator is 2. My numerator is 3. Write me down, and draw pictures that show
   (a) one whole, and (b) me.

J. Task: More or Less Than $1\frac{1}{2}$ (URG p. 17)

1. I am $\frac{1}{2}$ more than $1\frac{1}{2}$. What number am I?
2. I am $\frac{1}{4}$ less than $1\frac{1}{2}$. What number am I?
3. I am $\frac{1}{4}$ more than $1\frac{1}{2}$. What number am I?

Teaching the Activity

Students build on their experiences with fractions. A situation familiar to students, sharing pizza fairly, is the context for investigating fractions in this activity. Like the pattern blocks, pizzas present an area model of fractions. Students solve problems and share their solutions and strategies with one another. As students work in pairs, they use manipulatives and drawings to solve the problems and they talk and write about their methods and solutions. This activity, like the others in this unit, emphasizes the development of concepts rather than procedures. Your role is to help students connect their thinking about fractions to written symbols and to become familiar with the applications of fractions in their everyday world.

To introduce the idea of fair shares, draw Figure 3 on the overhead and ask:

* *Is this a fair way to share a pizza?*

Most students will note that the pizza is cut into two parts that are not equal. Ask,

* *Is this pizza cut into halves?* (No)
* *Why not?* (The two parts are not equal.)

In other words, the division must be "fair." Some students may claim that the line cuts off one-fourth of the pizza. This provides an opportunity for discussing how to check that claim. (If the circle is drawn on an overhead, lay a transparency of *Centimeter Grid Paper* on top of it. Find the areas of the parts by counting square centimeters, and see if the small area is about one-fourth of the whole area.)

Have student pairs solve the problems on the *Pizza Problems* Activity Pages in the *Student Guide*. In **Questions 1–5,** one pizza is shared. These problems are written as a story about a single pizza being shared by two, then by four, then by eight people. This common situation—one item divided among several people—emphasizes one basic fraction idea in this unit: fair sharing. After students complete **Questions 1–5,** have them share their pictures, solutions, and strategies with the class. Ask:

* *When are the pieces the largest?* (When the pizza is shared among the fewest people.)
* *Which is larger, $\frac{1}{2}$ pizza or $\frac{1}{3}$ pizza?* ($\frac{1}{2}$ pizza, $\frac{1}{2} > \frac{1}{3}$)

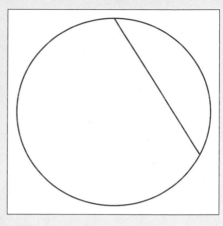

Figure 3: *A pizza cut into two parts*

Pizza Problems

Draw pictures, and then write words and fractions for your answers to these problems.

1. Mr. Davis is making one pizza for his two daughters, Cora and Felicia. If the two girls share the pizza fairly, then how much will each get?

2. Cora asks if her friend Tanya can stay for dinner. Felicia asks if her friend Erin can stay, too. Mr. Davis says both friends can stay. How much pizza will each of the four girls get?

3. Mr. Davis cuts the pizza into eight pieces. How many pieces will each girl get?

4. Just as the girls sit down to eat, Mrs. Davis gets home from work, Tanya's mother rings the doorbell, and Erin's mother calls on the telephone. Now, all four adults also want pizza. If everybody shares one pizza, then what fraction of the pizza will each person get?

5. Suppose your family shared one pizza fairly. What fraction of the pizza would each person get?

For Questions 6–11, it is best to work in a group with four people.

* Cut out paper circles to help you find the answers.
* Pretend the circles are pizzas, and share them fairly in your group.
* Draw pictures, and write words and fractions for your answers.

6. Amber, Alex, Denise, and Jason have a pizza they want to share fairly. How much pizza will each one get?

7. Four people share three pizzas fairly. How much pizza does each person get?

8. Four people share five pizzas fairly. How much does each person get?

9. Four people share six pizzas fairly. How much does each person get?

10. Four people share two and one-half pizzas fairly. How much does each person get?

Pizza Problems SG • Grade 3 • Unit 13 • Lesson 3 185

Student Guide - page 185 (Answers on p. 50)

If this is one whole pizza,

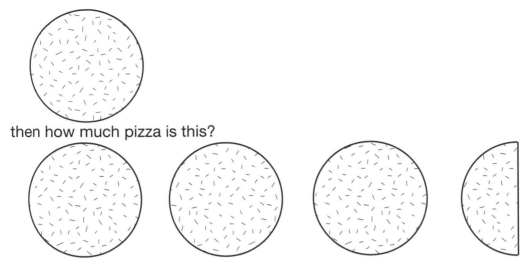

then how much pizza is this?

Figure 4: *A fraction greater than one whole*

In *Questions 6–11,* different numbers of pizzas are shared among four people so you may wish to use groups of four for these questions. Each pair needs scissors and several copies of the *Ten Pizzas* Blackline Master. Students pretend the paper circles are pizzas and share them fairly to solve the problems.

Before students attempt *Question 8,* make sure they know something about fractions greater than one whole. One way to do this is to display the problem shown in Figure 4. Students need to realize that three and a half, $\frac{7}{2}$, and $3\frac{1}{2}$ are all equivalent.

After students complete the problems, ask them to share their solutions and strategies. Expect and encourage a variety of strategies and solutions. For example, for *Question 10,* students may express the amount each person gets as $\frac{5}{8}$ of a pizza, but also expect and accept $\frac{1}{2} + \frac{1}{8}$. Figure 5 shows one possible solution strategy for *Question 10.*

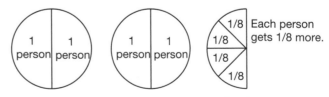

Each person gets 1/2 of a pizza and 1/8 of a pizza.
or
Each person gets 5/8 of a pizza.

Figure 5: *One solution strategy for Question 10*

In *Question 12,* the number of pizzas remains constant and the number of people varies. Five pizzas are shared among more and more people. Discuss the fact that the more people share the same number of pizzas, the less pizza each person gets: As the number of shares increases, the size of each share decreases. To solve these problems, students need scissors and several more copies of the *Ten Pizzas* Blackline Master.

Homework and Practice

- You can assign the Homework section on the *Pizza Problems* Activity Pages in the *Student Guide* at any time during this unit. The problems ask students to collect a variety of fractions from various sources. Post interesting fractions on a bulletin board.

- You can assign some or all of the problems in Lesson 5 *Fraction Problems* for homework as appropriate.

- DPP Bit G reviews the *Kid Fractions* activity. Task H provides practice with identifying fractions given the numerator and the denominator. Bit I asks students to skip count by halves and fourths. Task J builds number sense for fractions.

- Part 3 of the Home Practice provides practice with fractions using a clock face.

Answers for Part 3 of the Home Practice are in the Answer Key at the end of this lesson and at the end of this unit.

11. Make up your own number of pizzas to share fairly four ways. How much would each person get?

12. These problems are about sharing five pizzas with more and more people.
    - Copy the table on your own paper.
    - Use paper circles to help you complete the third column.
    - Draw pictures and write words and fractions to show your answers.

Number of People	Number of Pizzas	How much pizza does each person get?
2	5	
4	5	
5	5	
10	5	
20	5	

Student Guide - page 186 (Answers on p. 50)

Use the *Observational Assessment Record* to note whether students can represent fractions using drawings, words, and symbols.

Literature Connection

- Mathews, Louise. *Gator Pie*. Sundance Publishing, Littleton, MA, 1995.

  In this story, two alligators ("gators"), Alvin and Alice, find a pie. To share the pie fairly, each alligator would get half. Then more alligators arrive. Alvin and Alice must divide the pie into more pieces. As more and more alligators arrive, the piece that each alligator will receive becomes smaller. The alligators start to argue about sharing the pie. Finally, Alvin and Alice take the pie and sneak away.

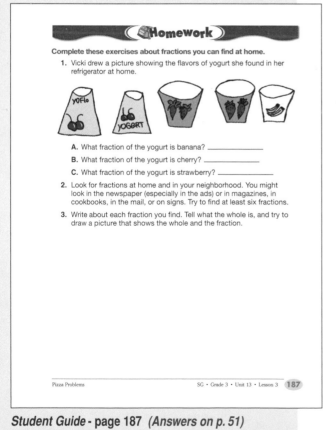

Homework

Complete these exercises about fractions you can find at home.

1. Vicki drew a picture showing the flavors of yogurt she found in her refrigerator at home.

   A. What fraction of the yogurt is banana? _____
   B. What fraction of the yogurt is cherry? _____
   C. What fraction of the yogurt is strawberry? _____

2. Look for fractions at home and in your neighborhood. You might look in the newspaper (especially in the ads) or in magazines, in cookbooks, in the mail, or on signs. Try to find at least six fractions.

3. Write about each fraction you find. Tell what the whole is, and try to draw a picture that shows the whole and the fraction.

Pizza Problems   SG • Grade 3 • Unit 13 • Lesson 3   **187**

Student Guide - page 187 *(Answers on p. 51)*

Name _____ Date _____

PART 3

Use a clock and a calculator to help you solve these problems.

How many minutes are there in:

1. 2 hours? _____
2. $1\frac{1}{2}$ hours? _____
3. $1\frac{1}{4}$ hours? _____
4. $1\frac{3}{4}$ hours? _____
5. $2\frac{1}{2}$ hours? _____

PART 4

Use what you know about quarters and $\frac{1}{4}$s to solve these problems. Tell how much money you would have after adding or subtracting these amounts.

1. You have 25¢ more than $2.50. _____
2. You have 25¢ less than $2.50. _____
3. You have 50¢ more than $2.50. _____
4. You have $1.50 more than $3.50. _____
5. You have $2.00 less than $3.75. _____

PART 5

Solve the problems. Estimate to be sure your answers are reasonable.

1.	2.	3.	4.
4006	4006	7032	7032
+498	−498	+1777	−1779

5. Explain your estimation strategy for Question 2.

PARTS AND WHOLES   DAB • Grade 3 • Unit 13 **195**

Discovery Assignment Book - page 195 *(Answers on p. 51)*

At a Glance

Math Facts and Daily Practice and Problems

DPP items G–J review and practice fraction concepts.

Teaching the Activity

1. Draw a circle on the board or overhead and divide it into two unequal parts.
2. Ask, *"If I cut a pizza like this, would I be sharing it equally?"*
3. Students discuss the problem and "fair shares."
4. Distribute four copies of *Ten Pizzas* Blackline Master to each pair.
5. Have student pairs solve the problems in *Questions 1–5* on the *Pizza Problems* Activity Pages in the *Student Guide* and share their pictures, solutions, and strategies with the class.
6. Students work in groups of four and use the paper pizzas to solve *Questions 6–12.*
7. Ask students to share their solutions and strategies. Expect and encourage a variety of solutions and strategies.

Homework

1. Assign the Homework section of the *Pizza Problems* Activity Pages.
2. Assign problems from the *Fraction Problems* Activity Pages (optional Lesson 5) as appropriate.
3. Assign Home Practice Part 3.

Assessment

Use the *Observational Assessment Record* to note students' abilities to represent fractions in pictures, words, and symbols.

Connection

Read and discuss *Gator Pie* by Louise Mathews.

Answer Key is on pages 50–51.

Notes:

Ten Pizzas

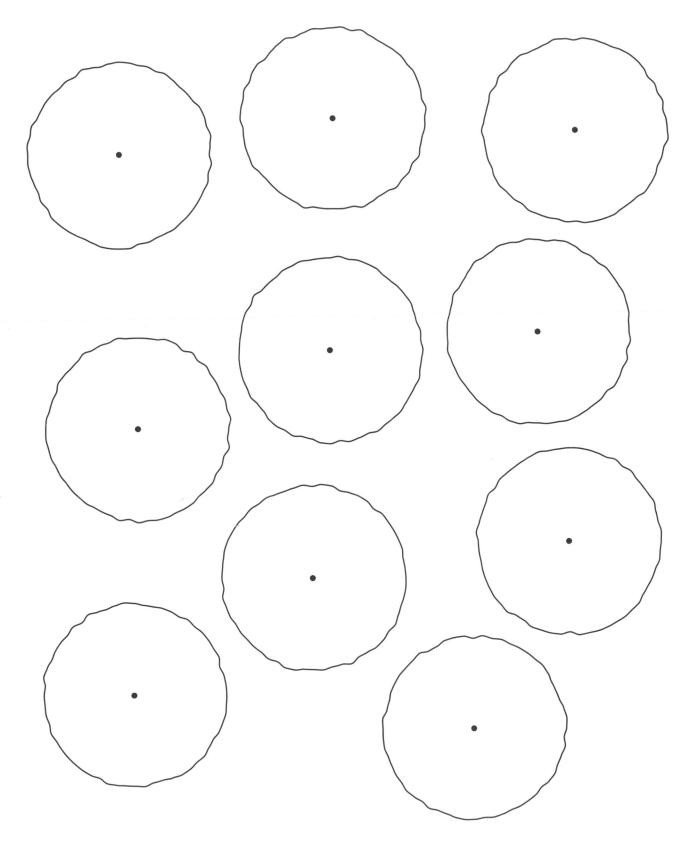

Name _____ Date _____

Centimeter Grid Paper, Blackline Master

Pizza Problems

Draw pictures, and then write words and fractions for your answers to these problems.

1. Mr. Davis is making one pizza for his two daughters, Cora and Felicia. If the two girls share the pizza fairly, then how much will each get?

2. Cora asks if her friend Tanya can stay for dinner. Felicia asks if her friend Erin can stay, too. Mr. Davis says both friends can stay. How much pizza will each of the four girls get?

3. Mr. Davis cuts the pizza into eight pieces. How many pieces will each girl get?

4. Just as the girls sit down to eat, Mrs. Davis gets home from work, Tanya's mother rings the doorbell, and Erin's mother calls on the telephone. Now, all four adults also want pizza. If everybody shares one pizza, then what fraction of the pizza will each person get?

5. Suppose your family shared one pizza fairly. What fraction of the pizza would each person get?

For Questions 6–11, it is best to work in a group with four people.

- Cut out paper circles to help you find the answers.
- Pretend the circles are pizzas, and share them fairly in your group.
- Draw pictures, and write words and fractions for your answers.

6. Amber, Alex, Denise, and Jason have a pizza they want to share fairly. How much pizza will each one get?

7. Four people share three pizzas fairly. How much pizza does each person get?

8. Four people share five pizzas fairly. How much does each person get?

9. Four people share six pizzas fairly. How much does each person get?

10. Four people share two and one-half pizzas fairly. How much does each person get?

Pizza Problems · SG • Grade 3 • Unit 13 • Lesson 3 · **185**

Student Guide - page 185

11. Make up your own number of pizzas to share fairly four ways. How much would each person get?

12. These problems are about sharing five pizzas with more and more people.

- Copy the table on your own paper.
- Use paper circles to help you complete the third column.
- Draw pictures and write words and fractions to show your answers.

Number of People	Number of Pizzas	How much pizza does each person get?
2	5	
4	5	
5	5	
10	5	
20	5	

186 SG • Grade 3 • Unit 13 • Lesson 3 · Pizza Problems

Student Guide - page 186

Student Guide (p. 185)

Pizza Problems*

1. $\frac{1}{2}$ pizza

2. $\frac{1}{4}$ pizza

3. 2 pieces

4. $\frac{1}{8}$ pizza

5. Answers will vary.

6. $\frac{1}{4}$ pizza

7. $\frac{3}{4}$ of a pizza ($\frac{1}{4}$ of each pizza)

8. $1\frac{1}{4}$ pizzas or ($\frac{5}{4}$ pizza)

9. $1\frac{1}{2}$ pizzas or ($\frac{6}{4}$ pizza)

10. $\frac{5}{8}$ of a pizza or $\frac{1}{2}$ of a pizza $+ \frac{1}{8}$ of a pizza (See Figure 5 in the Lesson Guide.)

Student Guide (p. 186)

11. Answers will vary.

12. $2\frac{1}{2}$ pizzas, $1\frac{1}{4}$ pizzas, 1 pizza, $\frac{1}{2}$ pizza, $\frac{1}{4}$ pizza

*Answers and/or discussion are included in the Lesson Guide.

Student Guide (p. 187)

Homework

1. A. $\frac{1}{5}$
   B. $\frac{2}{5}$
   C. $\frac{2}{5}$

2.–3. Answers will vary. Share pictures with the class.

Student Guide - page 187

Discovery Assignment Book (p. 195)

Home Practice*

Part 3

1. 120 minutes
2. 90 minutes
3. 75 minutes
4. 105 minutes
5. 150 minutes

Discovery Assignment Book - page 195

*Answers for all the Home Practice in the *Discovery Assignment Book* are at the end of the unit.

Lesson 4

Fraction Games

Lesson Overview

In *FractionLand,* students advance tokens along a path by answering questions involving fractions. The game's purpose is to practice finding a fraction of a whole number (such as $\frac{1}{2}$ of 16) by using beans or other counters.

In *Fraction Problem Game,* students compare two fractions and say a number sentence to move their pieces.

Key Content

- Finding fractional parts of sets.
- Finding fractional parts of whole numbers.
- Comparing and ordering fractions using counters.
- Comparing and ordering fractions using one-half as a benchmark.

Math Facts

DPP Bit K is the quiz on the square numbers.

Homework

1. Students play the games at home.
2. Assign Parts 1 and 2 of the Home Practice.

Assessment

1. Use DPP Bit K to assess students' fluency with multiplication facts for the square numbers.
2. Use the *Observational Assessment Record* to document students' abilities to find fractions of sets and to compare and order fractions.
3. Transfer appropriate documentation from the *Observational Assessment Record* to students' *Individual Assessment Record Sheets*.

Materials List

Supplies and Copies

Student	Teacher
Supplies for Each Student • envelope for storing flash cards • scissors • 50 counters (e.g., connecting cubes or beans) • game token **Supplies for Each Student Group** • clear plastic spinner (or pencil with paper clip)	**Supplies**
Copies	**Copies/Transparencies**

All blackline masters including assessment, transparency, and DPP masters are also on the Teacher Resource CD.

Student Books
Fraction Games (*Student Guide* Pages 188–189)
FractionLand Whole Number Deck (*Discovery Assignment Book* Page 201)
FractionLand Fraction Deck (*Discovery Assignment Book* Page 203)
FractionLand Game Board (*Discovery Assignment Book* Page 205)
Fraction Problem Game Fraction Cards (*Discovery Assignment Book* Page 207)
Fraction Problem Game Helper (*Discovery Assignment Book* Page 209)
Problem Game Board (*Discovery Assignment Book* Page 211)
Problem Game Spinner (*Discovery Assignment Book* Page 213)

Daily Practice and Problems and Home Practice
DPP items K–L (*Unit Resource Guide* Page 17)
Home Practice Parts 1–2 (*Discovery Assignment Book* Page 194)

Note: Classrooms whose pacing differs significantly from the suggested pacing of the units should use the Math Facts Calendar in Section 4 of the *Facts Resource Guide* to ensure students receive the complete math facts program.

Assessment Tools
Observational Assessment Record (*Unit Resource Guide* Pages 9–10)
Individual Assessment Record Sheet (*Teacher Implementation Guide,* Assessment section)

Suggestions for using the DPPs are on page 58.

K. Bit: Quiz on the Square Numbers
   (URG p. 17)

A. $4 \times 4 =$ B. $7 \times 7 =$
C. $1 \times 1 =$ D. $10 \times 10 =$
E. $3 \times 3 =$ F. $5 \times 5 =$
G. $6 \times 6 =$ H. $8 \times 8 =$
I. $9 \times 9 =$ J. $2 \times 2 =$

L. Task: Time Fractions (URG p. 17)

How many minutes in

1. 1 hour?
2. $\frac{1}{4}$ hour?
3. $\frac{1}{2}$ hour?
4. $\frac{3}{4}$ hour?
5. $1\frac{1}{2}$ hours?

Use a clock and a calculator to help you.

Before the Games

The first time *FractionLand* is played, the cards in the *Discovery Assignment Book* on the *FractionLand Whole Number Deck* and the *FractionLand Fraction Deck* Game Pages must be cut apart. Once the decks are cut apart, store each student's cards in an envelope.

Before playing the *Fraction Problem Game,* cut apart the cards on the *Fraction Problem Game Fraction Cards* Game Page. Students can store their cards in an envelope.

Part 1 *FractionLand*

Playing *FractionLand* requires solving such problems as "What is $\frac{1}{3}$ of 18?" Although students have encountered similar problems since first grade, they may still be difficult for many students. Work through several examples before students play the game.

Students should use counters to solve the problems. For example, to find $\frac{3}{4}$ of 12, a student might first divide the beans into four equal groups, and then count the beans in three of the four groups. By posing and discussing such problems, you prepare students for the game. Since students lose their turn if the answer is not even (such as $\frac{1}{4}$ of 9), be sure to include several such problems.

Fraction Games

FractionLand

In this game, a player picks a fraction card and a whole number card. Then he or she finds the number that is that fraction of the whole number.

Players

This is a game for two or more players.

Materials

- a token for each player
- a game board
- 1 deck of *FractionLand Whole Number* cards
- 1 deck of *FractionLand Fraction* cards
- 50 connecting cubes, beans, or other counters

Rules

1. Shuffle both decks separately. Put them face down next to each other.
2. Put the players' tokens on the Start rectangle.
3. Choose a player to go first.
4. Turn over the top card in each deck. One card shows a fraction; the other shows a whole number. Find the fraction of the whole number. Use the counters to help. For example, if you turn up $\frac{1}{2}$ and 12, then divide a group of 12 counters in half. Count the number in each group to find 1/2 of 12. If the answer doesn't come out even (for example, $\frac{1}{4}$ of 9), then you lose your turn.
5. Your answer is the number of squares you can now move forward.
6. Follow any instructions on the square where you land.
7. The first to reach the Finish rectangle (or beyond) is the winner.

188 SG • Grade 3 • Unit 13 • Lesson 4   Fraction Games

Student Guide - page 188

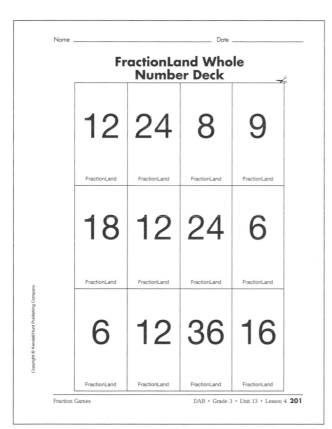

Discovery Assignment Book - page 201

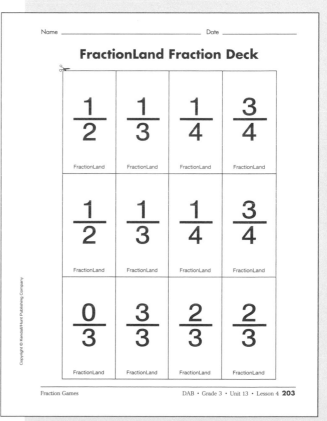

Discovery Assignment Book - page 203

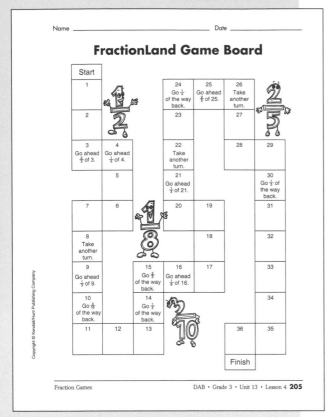

Discovery Assignment Book - page 205

Fraction Problem Game

Players

This is a game for two or more players.

Materials

- a game board
- problem cards
- scratch paper for writing answers
- a clear spinner or a paper clip and a pencil
- a token for each player
- *Fraction Problem Game Helper* page

Rules

1. Put the spinner over the spinner base on the *Problem Game Spinner* Game Page. (Or use a pencil and paper clip as a spinner.)
2. Put the problem cards on the Problem Cards rectangle.
3. Put everyone's token in the Start rectangle.
4. Spin to see who goes first.
5. When it is your turn, take the top card on the Problem Card stack. Compare the two fractions and say a number sentence describing them, using "greater than," "less than," or "equal to." Then write a number sentence using <, >, or =. If you are wrong, then your turn is over.
6. Use the *Fraction Problem Game Helper* page to help you solve the problems.
7. If you are right, spin the spinner, and move that many spaces.
8. Follow any directions on the space you land on. Sometimes, arrows help you move forward or make you move back.
9. Put the Problem Card on the Discard rectangle.
10. The first player to reach the Finish rectangle (or beyond) is the winner.

This game can be used with different card sets. Your teacher will help you understand what kind of problems you will solve for each card set.

Fraction Games   SG • Grade 3 • Unit 13 • Lesson 4 **189**

Student Guide - page 189

FractionLand is a game for two or more students. Each group needs only one set of the game cards. Introduce the game by reading and discussing the *FractionLand Rules* in the *Student Guide.* Students draw one card from each of two decks: One card will have a fraction; the other will have a whole number. Students move forward the fractional part of the given whole number on the *FractionLand Game Board* Game Page. For example, suppose a student pulls $\frac{1}{3}$ and 18. Since $\frac{1}{3}$ of 18 is 6, the student moves ahead six spaces. Some spaces have special instructions, most of which also involve fractions.

TIMS Tip

Students need some type of counters to play *FractionLand.* They can use connecting cubes by making a long train of cubes for the given number, and breaking the train into the number of (equal) parts indicated by the denominator of the given fraction. Students count the number of cubes in a part to find their answers.

Part 2 *Fraction Problem Game*

Students identify which of two fractions is larger and write and say a number sentence as their answer. Pose fraction comparison problems for students to solve before playing the game. Students can use the *Fraction Problem Game Helper* Game Page to help with their comparisons. Provide a variety of problems including: same numerator/different denominators, different numerators/same denominator, comparisons with one-half, and fractions on either side of one-half. Discuss each type of problem and review the symbols < and >. Encourage students to tell their methods for identifying the larger of two fractions. Discuss their strategies.

Introduce the game by reading and discussing the rules on the *Fraction Problem Game Rules* Game Page. Each group needs only one set of game cards. The *Problem Game Board* and the *Problem Game Spinner* are the same as those used in Unit 10. There are two fractions on each game card. The player needs to say and write a number sentence comparing the two fractions (e.g., $\frac{1}{2} < \frac{3}{5}$). If a player answers a problem correctly, he or she spins the spinner and advances his or her token. The problems are given on the *Fraction Problem Game Fraction Cards* Game Page.

The problem cards for this game do not have answers, so players will have to agree among themselves whether a given answer is correct or not. They can use the *Fraction Problem Game Helper* Game Page to show an answer is correct or to prove it wrong.

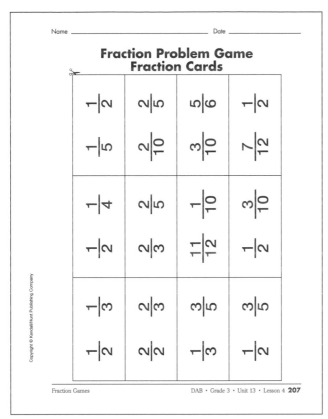

Discovery Assignment Book - page 207

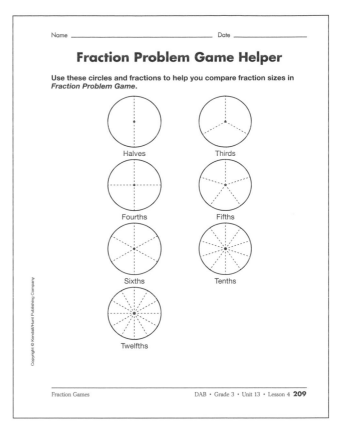

Discovery Assignment Book - page 209

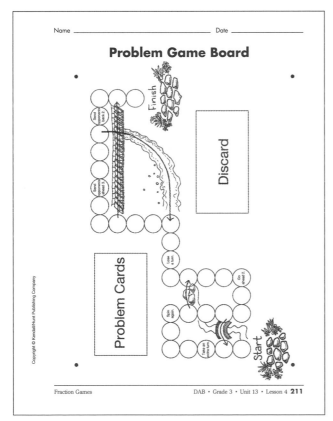

Discovery Assignment Book - page 211

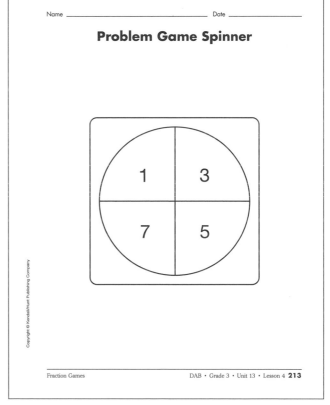

Discovery Assignment Book - page 213

Homework and Practice

- After students play the games in class, they can take them home as homework. Students will need counters, such as beans or coins, to play *FractionLand*.

- For DPP Task L students find fractions of hours in minutes.

- You can assign Parts 1 and 2 of the Home Practice as homework. Part 1 is similar to the *FractionLand* game in that students find fractions of sets. Part 2 asks students to skip count by thirds.

Answers for Parts 1 and 2 of the Home Practice are in the Answer Key at the end of this lesson and at the end of this unit.

Assessment

- DPP Bit K is the quiz on the square numbers.

- Use the *Observational Assessment Record* to document students' abilities to identify fractional parts of a set and to compare and order fractions.

- Transfer appropriate documentation from the Unit 13 *Observational Assessment Record* to students' *Individual Assessment Record Sheets*.

Extension

Students can create new game rules for *FractionLand* as they become familiar with the game. A good alternative to the rule that a player turning up a fraction of a whole number that is not "even" loses a turn is to have players use the nearest whole number instead. For example, $\frac{1}{4}$ of 9 would provide a move of 2.

At a Glance

Math Facts and Daily Practice and Problems

DPP Bit K is the quiz on the square numbers. For Task L students find fractions of hours in minutes.

Part 1. *FractionLand*

1. Students cut apart the game cards on the *FractionLand Whole Number Deck* and the *FractionLand Fraction Deck* Game Pages in the *Discovery Assignment Book.*
2. Students use counters to practice solving fraction problems, such as $\frac{1}{3}$ of 18 and $\frac{1}{4}$ of 9.
3. Read and discuss the rules for *FractionLand* in the *Student Guide.*
4. Students play *FractionLand.*

Part 2. *Fraction Problem Game*

1. Students cut apart the game cards on the *Fraction Problem Game Fraction Cards* Game Page in the *Discovery Assignment Book.*
2. Students practice comparing fraction sizes using the *Fraction Problem Game Helper* Game Page.
3. Read and discuss the rules for *Fraction Problem Game* in the *Student Guide.*
4. Students play *Fraction Problem Game.*

Homework

1. Students play the games at home.
2. Assign Parts 1 and 2 of the Home Practice.

Assessment

1. Use DPP Bit K to assess students' fluency with multiplication facts for the square numbers.
2. Use the *Observational Assessment Record* to document students' abilities to find fractions of sets and to compare and order fractions.
3. Transfer appropriate documentation from the *Observational Assessment Record* to students' *Individual Assessment Record Sheets.*

Extension

Have students create new game rules for *FractionLand.*

Answer Key is on page 60.

Notes:

Name _____ Date _____

Unit 13 Home Practice

PART 1

1. Ms. O'Neil has 25 students in her third-grade class. One-fifth go home for lunch, two-fifths bring a sack lunch, and two-fifths buy a hot lunch at school. Use beans or other counters to help you.
   A. What number of students go home for lunch? _____
   B. What number of students bring a lunch to school? _____
   C. What number of students buy a lunch at school? _____

2. Mr. Dwyer has 24 students in his third-grade class. 1/4 take the bus to school, 2/4 walk to school, and 1/4 get a ride in a car.
   A. What number of students take the bus to school? _____
   B. What number of students walk to school? _____
   C. What number of students get a ride in a car? _____

PART 2

1. Skip count by thirds to 10. Write the numbers.

| $\frac{1}{3}$ | $\frac{1}{3}$ | $\frac{1}{3}$ | $\frac{1}{3}$ | $\frac{1}{3}$ | $\frac{1}{3}$ | $\frac{1}{3}$ | $\frac{1}{3}$ | $\frac{1}{3}$ |

$\frac{1}{3}$ $\frac{2}{3}$ 1 $1\frac{1}{3}$ $1\frac{2}{3}$ 2 $2\frac{1}{3}$ $2\frac{2}{3}$ 3

_____

_____

2. I am $\frac{1}{3}$ more than 1. What number am I? _____
3. I am $\frac{1}{3}$ less than 1. What number am I? _____
4. I am $\frac{1}{3}$ more than $1\frac{1}{3}$. What number am I? _____
5. I am $\frac{1}{3}$ more than $1\frac{2}{3}$. What number am I? _____

Copyright © Kendall/Hunt Publishing Company

194 DAB • Grade 3 • Unit 13   PARTS AND WHOLES

Discovery Assignment Book - page 194

Discovery Assignment Book (p. 194)

Home Practice*

Part 1

1. A. 5 go home
   B. 10 bring a lunch
   C. 10 buy a lunch
2. A. 6 take the bus
   B. 12 walk
   C. 6 ride in a car

Part 2

1. $\frac{1}{3}, \frac{2}{3}, 1, 1\frac{1}{3}, 1\frac{2}{3}, 2, 2\frac{1}{3}, \ldots$
2. $1\frac{1}{3}$
3. $\frac{2}{3}$
4. $1\frac{2}{3}$
5. 2

---

*Answers for all the Home Practice in the *Discovery Assignment Book* are at the end of the unit.

Fraction Problems

Lesson Overview

This lesson is a set of word problems that builds on the fraction concepts in this unit.

Key Content

- Recognizing that fractional parts of a whole must be equal.
- Identifying fractional parts of a set.
- Solving fraction problems involving time.

Homework

Assign some or all of the problems for homework.

Materials List

Supplies and Copies

Student	Teacher
Supplies for Each Student • counters • calculator • clock face, optional	**Supplies**
Copies	**Copies/Transparencies**

All blackline masters including assessment, transparency, and DPP masters are also on the Teacher Resource CD.

Student Books

Fraction Problems (*Student Guide* Pages 190–191)

Teaching the Activity

This lesson is a set of word problems that gives students practice analyzing word problems critically and choosing appropriate methods for solving them. The problems strengthen students' understanding of the fraction concepts studied in this unit. Students identify fractional parts of shapes and sets.

Using the Problems. Students can work on the problems individually, in pairs, or in groups. One approach is to ask students to work on the problems individually at first and then to come together in pairs or small groups to compare solutions. Then the group's solutions can be shared with others in a class discussion. Because this activity does not require much teacher preparation, it is appropriate for a substitute teacher.

Students may need counters and a clock face to complete this set of problems. For *Questions 1A–F* students determine whether divided shapes show fourths. To answer the questions, they must understand the meaning of denominator and that fractional parts must have equal areas. In *Question 2* students find a fractional part when the whole is given. In *Question 3* they find the whole when the fractional part is given. *Questions 4–7* ask students to find fractional parts of hours, giving their answers in minutes. Students may need calculators to divide 60 minutes. *Question 8* requires students to analyze a diagram showing addition of two fractions and determine whether the answer given is correct. Several fractional concepts are required to answer this question, including defining the whole and understanding denominators.

Homework and Practice

You may assign some or all of the problems on the *Fraction Problems* Activity Pages in the *Student Guide* as homework.

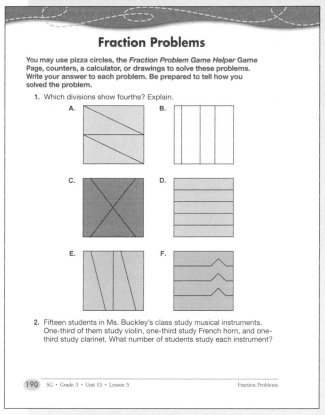

Student Guide - page 190 (Answers on p. 65)

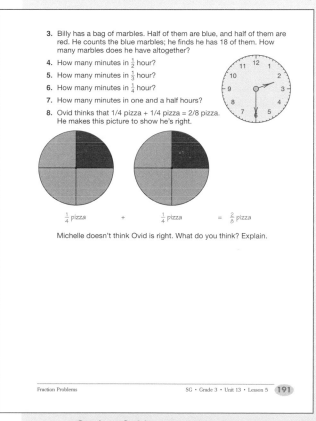

Student Guide - page 191 (Answers on p. 65)

Estimated Class Sessions

1

At a Glance

Teaching the Activity

1. Students solve the word problems on the *Fraction Problems* Activity Pages in the *Student Guide.*
2. Students discuss solutions and solution strategies.

Homework

Assign some or all of the problems for homework.

Answer Key is on page 65.

Notes:

Student Guide (p. 190)

Fraction Problems

1. A and E
   (B and C have four parts, but the parts are not equal sizes.)
   (D has 5 parts not 4.)
   (The two middle parts in F are equal but the top part is smaller in size and the bottom is larger.)

2. 5 students study each instrument.

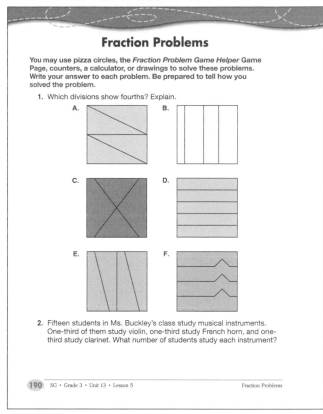

Student Guide - page 190

Student Guide (p. 191)

3. 36 marbles; 18 blue and 18 red

4. 30 minutes

5. 20 minutes

6. 15 minutes

7. 90 minutes

8. Ovid is incorrect. Ovid forgot the whole is made up of 4 equal pieces, not 8. The answer is $\frac{2}{4}$ or $\frac{1}{2}$.

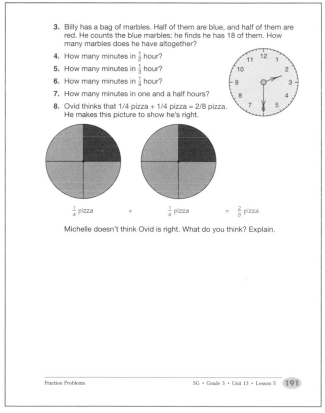

Student Guide - page 191

Name _____ Date _____

Unit 13 Home Practice

PART 1

1. Ms. O'Neil has 25 students in her third-grade class. One-fifth go home for lunch, two-fifths bring a sack lunch, and two-fifths buy a hot lunch at school. Use beans or other counters to help you.
   A. What number of students go home for lunch? _____
   B. What number of students bring a lunch to school? _____
   C. What number of students buy a lunch at school? _____

2. Mr. Dwyer has 24 students in his third-grade class. 1/4 take the bus to school, 2/4 walk to school, and 1/4 get a ride in a car.
   A. What number of students take the bus to school? _____
   B. What number of students walk to school? _____
   C. What number of students get a ride in a car? _____

PART 2

1. Skip count by thirds to 10. Write the numbers.

| $\frac{1}{3}$ | $\frac{1}{3}$ | $\frac{1}{3}$ | $\frac{1}{3}$ | $\frac{1}{3}$ | $\frac{1}{3}$ | $\frac{1}{3}$ | $\frac{1}{3}$ | $\frac{1}{3}$ |

$\frac{1}{3}$ $\frac{2}{3}$ 1 $1\frac{1}{3}$ $1\frac{2}{3}$ 2 $2\frac{1}{3}$ $2\frac{2}{3}$ 3

_____

2. I am $\frac{1}{3}$ more than 1. What number am I? _____
3. I am $\frac{1}{3}$ less than 1. What number am I? _____
4. I am $\frac{1}{3}$ more than $1\frac{1}{3}$. What number am I? _____
5. I am $\frac{1}{3}$ more than $1\frac{2}{3}$. What number am I? _____

194 DAB • Grade 3 • Unit 13   PARTS AND WHOLES

Discovery Assignment Book - page 194

Name _____ Date _____

PART 3

Use a clock and a calculator to help you solve these problems.
How many minutes are there in:

1. 2 hours? _____
2. $1\frac{1}{2}$ hours? _____
3. $1\frac{1}{4}$ hours? _____
4. $1\frac{3}{4}$ hours? _____
5. $2\frac{1}{2}$ hours? _____

PART 4

Use what you know about quarters and $\frac{1}{4}$s to solve these problems. Tell how much money you would have after adding or subtracting these amounts.

1. You have 25¢ more than $2.50. _____
2. You have 25¢ less than $2.50. _____
3. You have 50¢ more than $2.50. _____
4. You have $1.50 more than $3.50. _____
5. You have $2.00 less than $3.75. _____

PART 5

Solve the problems. Estimate to be sure your answers are reasonable.

1. 4006   2. 4006   3. 7032   4. 7032
   +498   −498   +1777   −1779

5. Explain your estimation strategy for Question 2.

PARTS AND WHOLES   DAB • Grade 3 • Unit 13 195

Discovery Assignment Book - page 195

Discovery Assignment Book (p. 194)

Part 1

1. A. 5 go home
   B. 10 bring a lunch
   C. 10 buy a lunch
2. A. 6 take the bus
   B. 12 walk
   C. 6 ride in a car

Part 2

1. $\frac{1}{3}, \frac{2}{3}, 1, 1\frac{1}{3}, 1\frac{2}{3}, 2, 2\frac{1}{3}, \ldots$
2. $1\frac{1}{3}$
3. $\frac{2}{3}$
4. $1\frac{2}{3}$
5. 2

Discovery Assignment Book (p. 195)

Part 3

1. 120 minutes
2. 90 minutes
3. 75 minutes
4. 105 minutes
5. 150 minutes

Part 4

1. $2.75
2. $2.25
3. $3.00
4. $5.00
5. $1.75

Part 5

1. 4504
2. 3508
3. 8809
4. 5253
5. Possible strategy: $4000 - 5000 = 3500$.

Glossary

This glossary provides definitions of key vocabulary terms in the Grade 3 lessons. Locations of key vocabulary terms in the curriculum are included with each definition. Components Key: URG = *Unit Resource Guide,* SG = *Student Guide,* and DAB = *Discovery Assignment Book.*

A

Area (URG Unit 5; SG Unit 5)
The area of a shape is the amount of space it covers, measured in square units.

Array (URG Unit 7 & Unit 11)
An array is an arrangement of elements into a rectangular pattern of (horizontal) rows and (vertical) columns. (*See* column and row.)

Associative Property of Addition (URG Unit 2)
For any three numbers $a, b,$ and c we have $a + (b + c) = (a + b) + c$. For example in finding the sum of 4, 8, and 2, one can compute $4 + 8$ first and then add 2: $(4 + 8) + 2 = 14$. Alternatively, we can compute $8 + 2$ and then add the result to 4: $4 + (8 + 2) = 4 + 10 = 14$.

Average (URG Unit 5)
A number that can be used to represent a typical value in a set of data. (*See also* mean and median.)

Axes (URG Unit 8; SG Unit 8)
Reference lines on a graph. In the Cartesian coordinate system, the axes are two perpendicular lines that meet at the origin. The singular of axes is axis.

B

Base (of a cube model) (URG Unit 18; SG Unit 18)
The part of a cube model that sits on the "ground."

Base-Ten Board (URG Unit 4)
A tool to help children organize base-ten pieces when they are representing numbers.

Base-Ten Pieces (URG Unit 4; SG Unit 4)
A set of manipulatives used to model our number system as shown in the figure at the right. Note that a skinny is made of 10 bits, a flat is made of 100 bits, and a pack is made of 1000 bits.

Base-Ten Shorthand (SG Unit 4)
A pictorial representation of the base-ten pieces as shown.

Nickname	Picture	Shorthand
bit		.
skinny		/
flat		
pack		

Best-Fit Line (URG Unit 9; SG Unit 9; DAB Unit 9)
The line that comes closest to the most number of points on a point graph.

Bit (URG Unit 4; SG Unit 4)
A cube that measures 1 cm on each edge. It is the smallest of the base-ten pieces that is often used to represent 1. (*See also* base-ten pieces.)

C

Capacity (URG Unit 16)
1. The volume of the inside of a container.
2. The largest volume a container can hold.

Cartesian Coordinate System (URG Unit 8)
A method of locating points on a flat surface by means of numbers. This method is named after its originator, René Descartes. (*See also* coordinates.)

Centimeter (cm)
A unit of measure in the metric system equal to one-hundredth of a meter. (1 inch = 2.54 cm)

Column (URG Unit 11)
In an array, the objects lined up vertically.

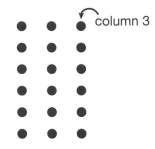
column 3

Common Fraction (URG Unit 15)
Any fraction that is written with a numerator and denominator that are whole numbers. For example, $\frac{3}{4}$ and $\frac{9}{4}$ are both common fractions. (*See also* decimal fraction.)

Commutative Property of Addition (URG Unit 2 & Unit 11)
This is also known as the Order Property of Addition. Changing the order of the addends does not change the sum. For example, $3 + 5 = 5 + 3 = 8$. Using variables, $n + m = m + n$.

Commutative Property of Multiplication (URG Unit 11)
Changing the order of the factors in a multiplication problem does not change the result, e.g., $7 \times 3 = 3 \times 7 = 21$. (*See also* turn-around facts.)

Congruent (URG Unit 12 & Unit 17; SG Unit 12)
Figures with the same shape and size.

Convenient Number (URG Unit 6)
A number used in computation that is close enough to give a good estimate, but is also easy to compute mentally, e.g., 25 and 30 are convenient numbers for 27.

Coordinates (URG Unit 8; SG Unit 8)
An ordered pair of numbers that locates points on a flat surface by giving distances from a pair of coordinate axes. For example, if a point has coordinates (4, 5) it is 4 units from the vertical axis and 5 units from the horizontal axis.

Counting Back (URG Unit 2)
A strategy for subtracting in which students start from a larger number and then count down until the number is reached. For example, to solve $8 - 3$, begin with 8 and count down three, 7, 6, 5.

Counting Down (*See* counting back.)

Counting Up (URG Unit 2)
A strategy for subtraction in which the student starts at the lower number and counts on to the higher number. For example, to solve $8 - 5$, the student starts at 5 and counts up three numbers (6, 7, 8). So $8 - 5 = 3$.

Cube (SG Unit 18)
A three-dimensional shape with six congruent square faces.

Cubic Centimeter (cc) (URG Unit 16; SG Unit 16)
The volume of a cube that is one centimeter long on each edge.

cubic centimeter

Cup (URG Unit 16)
A unit of volume equal to 8 fluid ounces, one-half pint.

D

Decimal Fraction (URG Unit 15)
A fraction written as a decimal. For example, 0.75 and 0.4 are decimal fractions and $\frac{75}{100}$ and $\frac{4}{10}$ are called common fractions. (*See also* fraction.)

Denominator (URG Unit 13)
The number below the line in a fraction. The denominator indicates the number of equal parts in which the unit whole is divided. For example, the 5 is the denominator in the fraction $\frac{2}{5}$. In this case the unit whole is divided into five equal parts.

Density (URG Unit 16)
The ratio of an object's mass to its volume.

Difference (URG Unit 2)
The answer to a subtraction problem.

Dissection (URG Unit 12 & Unit 17)
Cutting or decomposing a geometric shape into smaller shapes that cover it exactly.

Distributive Property of Multiplication over Addition (URG Unit 19)
For any three numbers a, b, and c, $a \times (b + c) = a \times b + a \times c$. The distributive property is the foundation for most methods of multidigit multiplication. For example, $9 \times (17) = 9 \times (10 + 7) = 9 \times 10 + 9 \times 7 = 90 + 63 = 153$.

E

Equal-Arm Balance
See two-pan balance.

Equilateral Triangle (URG Unit 7)
A triangle with all sides of equal length and all angles of equal measure.

Equivalent Fractions (SG Unit 17)
Fractions that have the same value, e.g., $\frac{2}{4} = \frac{1}{2}$.

Estimate (URG Unit 5 & Unit 6)
1. (verb) To find *about* how many.
2. (noun) An approximate number.

Extrapolation (URG Unit 7)
Using patterns in data to make predictions or to estimate values that lie beyond the range of values in the set of data.

F

Fact Family (URG Unit 11; SG Unit 11)
Related math facts, e.g., $3 \times 4 = 12$, $4 \times 3 = 12$, $12 \div 3 = 4$, $12 \div 4 = 3$.

Factor (URG Unit 11; SG Unit 11)
1. In a multiplication problem, the numbers that are multiplied together. In the problem $3 \times 4 = 12$, 3 and 4 are the factors.
2. Whole numbers that can be multiplied together to get a number. That is, numbers that divide a number evenly, e.g., 1, 2, 3, 4, 6, and 12 are all the factors of 12.

Fewest Pieces Rule (URG Unit 4 & Unit 6; SG Unit 4)
Using the least number of base-ten pieces to represent a number. (*See also* base-ten pieces.)

Flat (URG Unit 4; SG Unit 4)
A block that measures 1 cm $\times$ 10 cm $\times$ 10 cm. It is one of the base-ten pieces that is often used to represent 100. (*See also* base-ten pieces.)

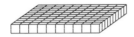

Flip (URG Unit 12)
A motion of the plane in which a figure is reflected over a line so that any point and its image are the same distance from the line.

Fraction (URG Unit 15)
A number that can be written as $\frac{a}{b}$ where a and b are whole numbers and b is not zero. For example, $\frac{1}{2}$, 0.5, and 2 are all fractions since 0.5 can be written as $\frac{5}{10}$ and 2 can be written as $\frac{2}{1}$.

Front-End Estimation (URG Unit 6)
Estimation by looking at the left-most digit.

G

Gallon (gal) (URG Unit 16)
A unit of volume equal to four quarts.

Gram
The basic unit used to measure mass.

H

Hexagon (SG Unit 12)
A six-sided polygon.

Horizontal Axis (SG Unit 1)
In a coordinate grid, the x-axis. The axis that extends from left to right.

I

Interpolation (URG Unit 7)
Making predictions or estimating values that lie between data points in a set of data.

J

K

Kilogram
1000 grams.

L

Likely Event (SG Unit 1)
An event that has a high probability of occurring.

Line of Symmetry (URG Unit 12)
A line is a line of symmetry for a plane figure if, when the figure is folded along this line, the two parts match exactly.

Line Symmetry (URG Unit 12; SG Unit 12)
A figure has line symmetry if it has at least one line of symmetry.

Liter (l) (URG Unit 16; SG Unit 16)
Metric unit used to measure volume. A liter is a little more than a quart.

M

Magic Square (URG Unit 2)
A square array of digits in which the sums of the rows, columns, and main diagonals are the same.

Making a Ten (URG Unit 2)
Strategies for addition and subtraction that make use of knowing the sums to ten. For example, knowing $6 + 4 = 10$ can be helpful in finding $10 - 6 = 4$ and $11 - 6 = 5$.

Mass (URG Unit 9 & Unit 16; SG Unit 9)
The amount of matter in an object.

Mean (URG Unit 5)
An average of a set of numbers that is found by adding the values of the data and dividing by the number of values.

Measurement Division (URG Unit 7)
Division as equal grouping. The total number of objects and the number of objects in each group are known. The number of groups is the unknown. For example, tulip bulbs come in packages of 8. If 216 bulbs are sold, how many packages are sold?

Measurement Error (URG Unit 9)
The unavoidable error that occurs due to the limitations inherent to any measurement instrument.

Median (URG Unit 5; DAB Unit 5)
For a set with an odd number of data arranged in order, it is the middle number. For an even number of data arranged in order, it is the number halfway between the two middle numbers.

Meniscus (URG Unit 16; SG Unit 16)
The curved surface formed when a liquid creeps up the side of a container (for example, a graduated cylinder).

Meter (m)
The standard unit of length measure in the metric system. One meter is approximately 39 inches.

Milliliter (ml) (URG Unit 16; SG Unit 16)
A measure of capacity in the metric system that is the volume of a cube that is one centimeter long on each edge.

Multiple (URG Unit 3 & Unit 11)
A number is a multiple of another number if it is evenly divisible by that number. For example, 12 is a multiple of 2 since 2 divides 12 evenly.

N

Numerator (URG Unit 13)
The number written above the line in a fraction. For example, the 2 is the numerator in the fraction $\frac{2}{5}$. (*See also* denominator.)

O

One-Dimensional Object (URG Unit 18; SG Unit 18)
An object is one-dimensional if it is made up of pieces of lines and curves.

Ordered Pairs (URG Unit 8)
A pair of numbers that gives the coordinates of a point on a grid in relation to the origin. The horizontal coordinate is given first; the vertical coordinate is given second. For example, the ordered pair (5, 3) tells us to move five units to the right of the origin and 3 units up.

Origin (URG Unit 8)
The point at which the *x*- and *y*-axes (horizontal and vertical axes) intersect on a coordinate plane. The origin is described by the ordered pair (0, 0) and serves as a reference point so that all the points on the plane can be located by ordered pairs.

P

Pack (URG Unit 4; SG Unit 4)
A cube that measures 10 cm on each edge. It is one of the base-ten pieces that is often used to represent 1000. (*See also* base-ten pieces.)

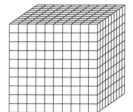

Palindrome (URG Unit 6)
A number, word, or phrase that reads the same forward and backward, e.g., 12321.

Parallel Lines (URG Unit 18)
Lines that are in the same direction. In the plane, parallel lines are lines that do not intersect.

Parallelogram (URG Unit 18)
A quadrilateral with two pairs of parallel sides.

Partitive Division (URG Unit 7)
Division as equal sharing. The total number of objects and the number of groups are known. The number of objects in each group is the unknown. For example, Frank has 144 marbles that he divides equally into 6 groups. How many marbles are in each group?

Pentagon (SG Unit 12)
A five-sided, five-angled polygon.

Perimeter (URG Unit 7; DAB Unit 7)
The distance around a two-dimensional shape.

Pint (URG Unit 16)
A unit of volume measure equal to 16 fluid ounces, i.e., two cups.

Polygon
A two-dimensional connected figure made of line segments in which each endpoint of every side meets with an endpoint of exactly one other side.

Population (URG Unit 1; SG Unit 1)
A collection of persons or things whose properties will be analyzed in a survey or experiment.

Prediction (SG Unit 1)
Using data to declare or foretell what is likely to occur.

Prime Number (URG Unit 11)
A number that has exactly two factors. For example, 7 has exactly two distinct factors, 1 and 7.

Prism
A three-dimensional figure that has two congruent faces, called bases, that are parallel to each other, and all other faces are parallelograms.

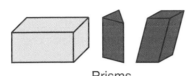
Prisms

Not a prism

Product (URG Unit 11; SG Unit 11; DAB Unit 11)
The answer to a multiplication problem. In the problem $3 \times 4 = 12$, 12 is the product.

Q

Quadrilateral (URG Unit 18)
A polygon with four sides.

Quart (URG Unit 16)
A unit of volume equal to 32 fluid ounces; one quarter of a gallon.

R

Recording Sheet (URG Unit 4)
A place value chart used for addition and subtraction problems.

Rectangular Prism (URG Unit 18; SG Unit 18)
A prism whose bases are rectangles. A right rectangular prism is a prism having all faces rectangles.

Regular (URG Unit 7; DAB Unit 7)
A polygon is regular if all sides are of equal length and all angles are equal.

Remainder (URG Unit 7)
Something that remains or is left after a division problem. The portion of the dividend that is not evenly divisible by the divisor, e.g., $16 \div 5 = 3$ with 1 as a remainder.

Right Angle (SG Unit 12)
An angle that measures 90°.

Rotation (turn) (URG Unit 12)
A transformation (motion) in which a figure is turned a specified angle and direction around a point.

Row (URG Unit 11)
In an array, the objects lined up horizontally.

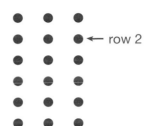
← row 2

Rubric (URG Unit 2)
A written guideline for assigning scores to student work, for the purpose of assessment.

S

Sample (URG Unit 1; SG Unit 1)
A part or subset of a population.

Skinny (URG Unit 4; SG Unit 4)
A block that measures 1 cm × 1 cm × 10 cm. It is one of the base-ten pieces that is often used to represent 10. (*See also* base-ten pieces.)

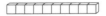

Square Centimeter (sq cm) (SG Unit 5)
The area of a square that is 1 cm long on each side.

Square Number (SG Unit 11)
A number that is the product of a whole number multiplied by itself. For example, 25 is a square number since $5 \times 5 = 25$. A square number can be represented by a square array with the same number of rows as columns. A square array for 25 has 5 rows of 5 objects in each row or 25 total objects.

Standard Masses
A set of objects with convenient masses, usually 1 g, 10 g, 100 g, etc.

Sum (URG Unit 2; SG Unit 2)
The answer to an addition problem.

Survey (URG Unit 14; SG Unit 14)
An investigation conducted by collecting data from a sample of a population and then analyzing it. Usually surveys are used to make predictions about the entire population.

T

Tangrams (SG Unit 12)
A type of geometric puzzle. A shape is given and it must be covered exactly with seven standard shapes called tans.

Thinking Addition (URG Unit 2)
A strategy for subtraction that uses a related addition problem. For example, $15 - 7 = 8$ because $8 + 7 = 15$.

Three-Dimensional (URG Unit 18; SG Unit 18)
Existing in three-dimensional space; having length, width, and depth.

TIMS Laboratory Method (URG Unit 1; SG Unit 1)
A method that students use to organize experiments and investigations. It involves four components: draw, collect, graph, and explore. It is a way to help students learn about the scientific method.

Turn (URG Unit 12)
(*See* rotation.)

Turn-Around Facts (URG Unit 2 & Unit 11 p. 37; SG Unit 11)
Addition facts that have the same addends but in a different order, e.g., $3 + 4 = 7$ and $4 + 3 = 7$. (*See also* commutative property of addition and commutative property of multiplication.)

Two-Dimensional (URG Unit 18; SG Unit 18)
Existing in the plane; having length and width.

Two-Pan Balance
A device for measuring the mass of an object by balancing the object against a number of standard masses (usually multiples of 1 unit, 10 units, and 100 units, etc.).

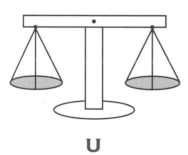

U

Unit (of measurement) (URG Unit 18)
A precisely fixed quantity used to measure. For example, centimeter, foot, kilogram, and quart are units of measurement.

Using a Ten (URG Unit 2)
1. A strategy for addition that uses partitions of the number 10. For example, one can find $8 + 6$ by thinking $8 + 6 = 8 + 2 + 4 = 10 + 4 = 14$.
2. A strategy for subtraction that uses facts that involve subtracting 10. For example, students can use $17 - 10 = 7$ to learn the "close fact" $17 - 9 = 8$.

Using Doubles (URG Unit 2)
Strategies for addition and subtraction that use knowing doubles. For example, one can find $7 + 8$ by thinking $7 + 8 = 7 + 7 + 1 = 14 + 1 = 15$. Knowing $7 + 7 = 14$ can be helpful in finding $14 - 7 = 7$ and $14 - 8 = 6$.

V

Value (URG Unit 1; SG Unit 1)
The possible outcomes of a variable. For example, red, green, and blue are possible values for the variable *color*. Two meters and 1.65 meters are possible values for the variable *length*.

Variable (URG Unit 1; SG Unit 1)
1. An attribute or quantity that changes or varies.
2. A symbol that can stand for a variable.

Vertex (URG Unit 12; SG Unit 12)
1. A point where the sides of a polygon meet.
2. A point where the edges of a three-dimensional object meet.

Vertical Axis (SG Unit 1)
In a coordinate grid, the *y*-axis. It is perpendicular to the horizontal axis.

Volume (URG Unit 16; SG Unit 16)
The measure of the amount of space occupied by an object.

Volume by Displacement (URG Unit 16)
A way of measuring volume of an object by measuring the amount of water (or some other fluid) it displaces.

W

Weight (URG Unit 9)
A measure of the pull of gravity on an object. One unit for measuring weight is the pound.

X

Y

Z